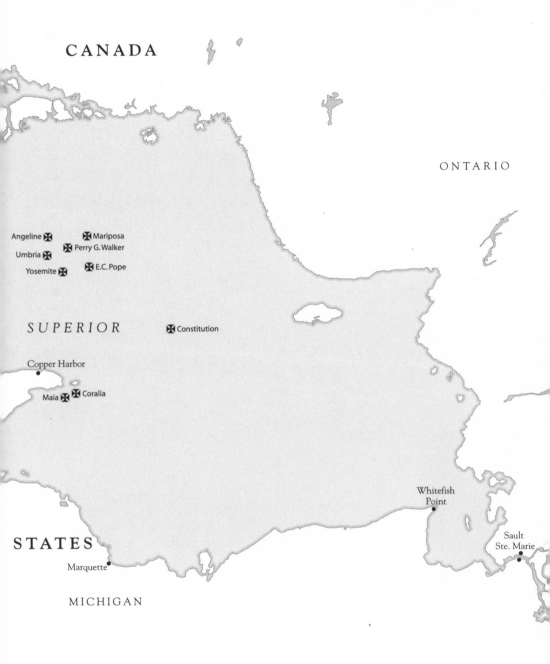

CANADA

ONTARIO

Angeline ⚓ ⚓ Mariposa
         ⚓ Perry G. Walker
Umbria ⚓
Yosemite ⚓ ⚓ E.C. Pope

SUPERIOR   ⚓ Constitution

Copper Harbor

Maia ⚓ ⚓ Coralia

Whitefish
Point

Sault
Ste. Marie

STATES

Marquette

MICHIGAN

So terrible a Storm

A Tale of Fury on Lake Superior

By Curt Brown

Voyageur Press

First published in 2008 by Voyageur Press, an imprint of MBI Publishing Company, 400 First Avenue North, Suite 300, Minneapolis, MN 55401 USA.

Voyageur Press titles are also available at discounts in bulk quantity for industrial or sales-promotional use. For details write to Special Sales Manager at MBI Publishing Company, 400 First Avenue North, Suite 300, Minneapolis, MN 55401 USA.

To find out more about our books, join us online at www.voyageurpress.com.

Library of Congress Cataloging-in-Publication Data

Brown, Curt, 1960-
    So terrible a storm : a tale of fury on Lake Superior / by Curt Brown.
        p. cm.
    Includes bibliographical references.
    ISBN 978-0-7603-3243-6 (hb w/jkt)
    1. Shipwrecks—Superior, Lake. 2. Mataafa (Steamship) I. Title.
    G525.B8573 2008
    917.74'90441—dc22

                                                                    2008000832

Edited by Danielle Ibister
Designed by Elly Gosso
Maps by Patti Isaacs, Parrot Graphics

Endpapers: Map of ships wrecked in the Lake Superior storm of November 27–29, 1905.

Page 1: An ore boat on Lake Superior's horizon, seen from Two Harbors. *Minnesota Historical Society*

Pages 6–7: Duluth piers in a 1906 storm. *Photo by Charles P. Gibson, Minnesota Historical Society*

Printed in the United States of America

To my lighthouses

Adele, Alison, Mackenzie, Zac, and Judy

"They are swept by Borean and dismasting blasts as direful as any that lash the salted wave; they know what shipwrecks are, for out of sight of land, however inland, they have drowned full many a midnight ship with all its shrieking crew."

~ Herman Melville
Moby-Dick, 1851

"Never in the history of Duluth has there been an incident so fraught with human interest, so compelling and absorbing."

~ Mary D. McFadden
Duluth News Tribune
December 10, 1905

"It has been a week that will always be remembered. It has been a week that children of today will tell their children's children about years hence. It has been a hard, harsh, heart-wringing period, and nothing can replace the manly lives that have been sacrificed on the altar of commerce to appease the wrath of the lake."

~ *Duluth Evening Herald*
December 2, 1905

Contents

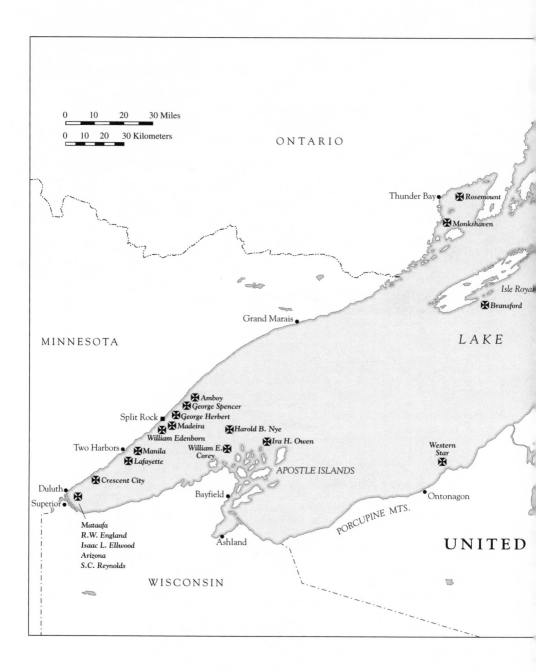

0   10   20   30 Miles

0   10   20   30 Kilometers

ONTARIO

Thunder Bay ● ✠ *Rosemount*

✠ *Monkshaven*

Isle Royal

✠ *Bransford*

Grand Marais ●

MINNESOTA

LAKE

✠ *Amboy*
✠ *George Spencer*

Split Rock ■ ✠ *George Herbert*
✠ *Madeira*

✠ *William Edenborn*   ✠ *Harold B. Nye*

Two Harbors ●   ✠ *Manila*   ✠ *William E.*   ✠ *Ira H. Owen*
✠ *Lafayette*   *Corey*

✠ *Crescent City*   *APOSTLE ISLANDS*

Western
Star
✠

Duluth ●
✠
Superior ●

Bayfield ●

● Ontonagon

Mataafa
R.W. England
Isaac L. Ellwood
Arizona
S.C. Reynolds

PORCUPINE MTS.

UNITED

Ashland ●

WISCONSIN

CANADA

ONTARIO

ngeline ✠ ✠ Mariposa
✠ Perry G. Walker
Umbria ✠
Yosemite ✠ ✠ E.C. Pope

SUPERIOR ✠ Constitution

Copper Harbor

Maia ✠✠ Coralia

Whitefish
Point

Sault
Ste. Marie

STATES
Marquette

MICHIGAN

Preface

"It is the most dangerous piece of water in the
whole world. Here winter falls in autumn,
and from then until late spring it is a region
of blizzards and blinding snowstorms. The
coasts are harborless wildernesses with . . .
reefs and rocky headlands that jut out like
knives to cut ships in two."

~ James Oliver Curwood
Early 1905

For me, this story started at the end. On a family trip up Lake Superior's North Shore, about fifty miles up Highway 61 from Duluth, Minnesota, we did what so many do. We pulled over to visit the Split Rock Lighthouse perched 178 feet up a rock cliff above the slate waters of Lake Superior. It could have been a tour guide in a straw boater hat mimicking the garb of a 1910 lighthouse keeper. Or simply a brochure. I don't recall.

I just know my curiosity was piqued when I learned this brick beacon on a lonely cliff was built in response to a nasty 1905 storm that battered nearly thirty boats and claimed more than thirty lives of sailors trapped on Lake Superior during three wind-howling, frigid days in late November.

Unlike most sailing journeys, which embark from a port's dock, this tale set sail during a trip to the cool marble inside the downtown library of St. Paul, Minnesota. A thick, dusty volume, with a light odor of mildew, carried an even thicker title: *The Great Lakes, the Vessels that Plough Them: Their Owners, Their Sailors, and Their Cargoes, Together with a Brief History of Our Inland Seas.*

Published in 1909, James Oliver Curwood's tome quickly and pointedly challenged me to write this book. The writer's century-old voice actually dared me.

"For some unaccountable reason," Curwood bemoans in his preface, "the Great Lakes . . . have been almost entirely neglected by writers."

"One of the most inexplainable mysteries of the century," he goes on, "exists in the fact that the Great Lakes of to-day are as little known to the vast majority of Americans as they were a quarter-century ago."

I grew up on Lake Michigan's North Shore in the Chicago suburb of Glencoe. But sitting in that library, this fat book open before me on a walnut table, I struggled to place the "Inland Seas" on my mental map. Never mind my college degrees in history and American studies. This long-dead writer was right. I didn't know Lake Huron from Lake Ontario. When I learned in my ensuing research that a bulk freighter named the *German* actually crashed on the Glencoe beach during the 1905 storm, I felt almost guilty about my ignorance. And Curwood's shaming picked up speed.

"America's great Inland Seas have remained unwatched and unknown except by a comparative few," he scolded. "Not one person in ten knows what the Great Lakes stand for to-day. While a thousand writers have sung of the greatness and romance of the watery wastes that encircle continents, none have told of those 'vast unsalted seas' . . . .

"Even of those who live in the states bordering the Great Lakes but few know that these fresh water highways possess . . . the elements of romance and tragedy."

He lightens up some, acknowledging that the boom of shipping on the Lakes grew fast around the turn of the twentieth century: "In a small way the general lack of knowledge is excusable, for the development has been so rapid and so stupendous that people have not yet grasped its significance."

Curwood spent twenty years sailing the Lakes and writing the history of their captains, their commerce, and their storms. He issued his challenge to me on page 92:

"I believe that the failure to treat of the human interest of the Lakes is one of the most inexcusable omissions in American literature. In the rush for modern progress the Lakes have been forgotten. . . . Historians, novelists and short-story writers have neglected the Lakes."

Curwood then rolled up his sleeves and pointed at me, the kid from Glencoe, and by extension my kids, who trek to the opening night screenings of Johnny Depp's latest pirate movies. Remember, he was writing in 1909.

"In this age, the youths of Chicago, Cincinnati, and Denver . . . search public libraries for tales of the South Seas and of the Great Pacific; even the youngster whose every day has been spent on the shores of the five Great Lakes seeks afar the material that satisfies his boyish imagination."

So the gauntlet was laid, the research begun, and my boyish imagination ignited. This book frames three days—November 27, 28, and 29—when Minnesota's most compelling weather story ever played out on Lake Superior's western coast and the burgeoning city of Duluth.

For those readers itching to set sail, turn now to Part 2. For those with the patience and thirst for context, stay with Part 1 for a condensed history of Lake Superior and its shipping industry. It will add richness to the narrative that follows.

Curt Brown

St. Paul, Minnesota

October 1, 2007

Thunder Bay

MINNESOTA

Lake Superior

Split Rock
Lighthouse (1910)

Duluth

Ashland

Edmund Fitzgerald (1975) ✠

Marquette

Sault Ste. Ma

M
I
C
H
I
G
A
N

WISCONSIN

Green Bay

Lake Michigan

Milwaukee

Grand Haven

Chicago

Gary

ILLINOIS

UNITED

STATES

INDIANA

Lake Superior Sites

Minnesota

Duluth: One of the world's busiest ports in 1905 and the vortex of the storm on November 27–29, 1905.

Split Rock Lighthouse: The barge *Madeira* crashed against Split Rock at the height of the storm. Nine crewmembers miraculously escaped the sinking ship. Opened in 1910, Split Rock Lighthouse is now one of Lake Superior's best known landmarks.

Wisconsin

Ashland: The steamship *Sir William Siemens* limped into Ashland after the storm and reported seeing wreckage of the *Ira H. Owen*.

Green Bay: In 1679, French explorer Rene-Robert de LaSalle's twin-masted boat, the *Griffon*, vanished near Green Bay with a load of fur pelts during the Great Lakes' first commercial shipping venture.

Illinois

Chicago: *Mataafa* oiler Carl Carlson's sister and chief engineer William Most's wife received news of their deaths in Chicago. The ore boat *German* beached off the North Shore village of Glencoe.

Indiana

Gary: Named after U.S. Steel chairman Elbert Gary, the city became an important Great Lakes port after 1906.

Michigan

Detroit: Two French priests passed through the Detroit River in 1670. Detroit remained the westernmost spot Buffalo steamers would venture through the 1830s.

Grand Haven: Home of *Ira H. Owen* captain Thomas Honner.

Lexington: Birthplace and burial location of steamer *Mataafa* captain Dick Humble.

Marquette: At first, it was believed Thomas Honner's brother, George, died in the storm, but he turned up safe in Marquette, mastering the *Fleetwood*.

Muskegon: The year before his death, Thomas Honner was mastering the steamer *City of Straits* between Chicago and Muskegon.

Sault Sainte Marie: Although the Hudson's Bay Company had built a small lock and sluice in the 1790s, Soo Locks canal construction at Sault Sainte Marie in 1855 opened up Lake Superior as never before.

Ohio

Ashtabula: Thanks to its proximity to Lake Erie and thirty miles of shoreline, Ashtabula was a major shipping center.

Conneaut: Home of *Mataafa* captain Dick Humble.

Wickliffe: Pittsburgh Steamship Company president Harry Coulby built a mansion in Wickliffe in 1913 and served as the village's first mayor.

Pennsylvania

Erie: Located halfway between Cleveland and Buffalo, Erie has long been a maritime and rail hub and grew into an industrial center through the manufacture of steel and iron.

New York

Buffalo: The other end of the thousand-mile watery highway from Duluth, Buffalo was the home of several sailors caught in the storm, including *Mataafa* engineer James Early, whose wife had just given birth to a baby daughter.

Ontario

Amherstburg: Home of the *Mataafa*'s three black crewmembers: cook Walter Bush, steward Henry Wright, and porter Fred Saunders.

Collingwood: Hometown of *Crescent City* watchman Arthur Daggett.

Hamilton: The steel industry prompted Hamilton's population to double between 1900 and 1914.

Thunder Bay: The 1905 storm's first victim, the *Monkshaven*, slammed into an island near Thunder Bay, but the crew climbed off the bow safely.

Toronto: *Mataafa* fireman Thomas Woodgate carried a letter from his father, a fruit seller back home in Toronto, worrying about stormy weather.

PART 1

Foreword

I

"Iron seemeth a simple metal, but in its nature
are many mysteries . . . and men who bend to
them their minds shall, in arriving days,
gather therefrom great profits not to
themselves alone but to all mankind."

~ Joseph Glanvill, 1668

"They lived in the lake country like deer
and foxes, leaving it unchanged by
their possession."

~ Walter Havighurst, 1966

The Great Lakes are pups, geologically speaking.

At least four distinct ice ages have sent glaciers crawling down from the polar ice cap to cover North America in the last 2.5 million years. And when the last of the glaciers melted off Lake Superior's North Shore ten thousand years ago, civilized, agricultural communities had already hatched across the globe in the Middle East towns near Jericho.

Before and between the ice ages, before the Great Lakes were born, a monstrous Laurentian River roared eastward through the high plains of a fledgling continent. The ice age glaciers ran two miles deep at points, some ten thousand feet of slow-moving ice that did more than blanket the northern regions in silence. The ice entombed a massive area. As the glaciers receded, they plugged up the old Laurentian riverbeds and drainage spots and gouged five giant bowls between what would become Duluth and Buffalo, some 1,200 miles to the east.

The surging water opened new channels, creating splendid elevation drops at Niagara Falls and leaving an unfathomable depth of sweet, fresh water overflowing the five large basins. The water in the Great Lakes could fill a ten-foot-deep swimming pool across the entire continental United States. The scooping of the retreating glaciers also created the planet's single largest freshwater pool. With nearly three thousand cubic miles of water volume, Lake

Superior contains more water than its four sisters combined. It covers 350 miles from Duluth to the glacial drainage blockage at Sault Sainte Marie, with depths of 1,300 feet at points. Its elevation of 600 feet also makes it higher than Lakes Huron, Michigan, Erie, and Ontario—which is why white people started calling it Superior. Native tribes had long before named it Gitchegomee.

Climatic conditions mellowed after the last of the glaciers puddled up ten thousand years ago, and forests emerged that were punctuated with game animals and fish. Indian nations, in turn, were drawn to the area: the Iroquois on Lake Ontario, the Algonquin on Lake Huron, and the Ojibwe, Cree, and Dakota around Lake Superior.

The native people respected the massive pools of water, venturing out to fish in birch bark canoes only in calm weather. They studied the storms and feared them, wisely clinging close to shore.

When white men arrived nearly four hundred years ago, the Lakes became something different: a conveyor belt of goods, a thousand-mile commercial highway.

II

"Twenty years ago Duluth was a little town with only a promising local trade. Today it's one of the great shipping ports of the world with unlimited possibilities of expansion."

~ James J. Hill, 1909

By the time the Mayflower bumped into Plymouth Rock in 1620, French explorers had already settled Quebec. Before long, they made their way across Lake Superior. From 1620 to 1720, a series of French swashbucklers and Jesuit missionaries snaked their way deep into the Great Lakes in birch bark canoes and flat-bottomed batteaux. They sought to claim New France for King Louis XIV.

Priests in long frock coats dipped quills into an inky mixture of gunpowder and snow to make crude maps and document tales of their often deadly missions into the raw wilderness. A desire to baptize curious Indians and satisfy the fashion demand for beaver fur hats pushed them west.

When Pierre-Esprit Radisson made a 1654 trek to the Head of the Lakes, as pre-Duluth was known, he returned bearing an armada of Indian canoes packed with pelts. Daniel Greysolon, Sieur DuLuth, made it to the Saint Louis River in 1679 before pushing on to Mille Lacs and

DANIEL GREYSOLON SIEUR DULHUT
AT THE HEAD OF THE LAKES — 1679

Daniel Greysolon, Sieur DuLuth, travels with Indians in 1679 at the Head of the Lakes, as pre-Duluth was known. *Artist: Francis Lee Jaques, Minnesota Historical Society*

the Mississippi. He befriended Cree, Ojibwe, and Dakota with trades of hatchets, kettles, knives, and guns. Soon, French trading posts dotted the lakeshores. The colorful songs of the voyageurs in their huge canoes broke the silence.

By the 1760s, the British had followed the French into the area. And by 1820, the exploring was over and the region had been mapped by U.S. surveyors such as Zebulon Pike, who then pressed on to the Rockies and the peak that bears his name. Other explorers became enchanted with Lake Superior. Henry Schoolcraft, his brother Jim, brother-in-law George Johnston, and a young doctor, Douglass Houghton—packing a vaccinating needle for the native tribes—journeyed to Lake Superior in 1831 with a Detroit printer and team of soldiers. Henry Schoolcraft called Superior the "blue profound" and became a diplomatic expert in Indian languages and lore—inspiring poet Henry Longfellow's "The Song of Hiawatha."

Schoolcraft had only one problem with Lake Superior: its name. Schoolcraft preferred the Ojibwe's moniker, Gitchegomee. But he acknowledged that was a mouthful. Schoolcraft launched a campaign to rename Superior Lake Algona, meaning "the seas of the Algonquins." His attempt was soon forgotten, but Schoolcraft never forgot his "blue profound."

In 1851, Schoolcraft, then 58 years old, penned his *Personal Memoirs of a Residence of Thirty Years on the American Frontiers*. In it, he correctly predicted Superior's future as a commercial catalyst:

Lake Superior lay before us. He who, for the first time, lifts his eyes upon this expanse, is amazed and delighted at its magnitude. Vastness is the term by which it is, more than any other, described. Clouds robed in sunshine, hanging in fleecy or nebular masses above—a bright pure illimitable plain of water—blue mountains or dim islands in the distance—a shore of green foliage on the one hand—a waste of waters on the other. These are the prominent objects on which the eye rests. We are diverted by the flight of birds, as on the ocean. A tiny sail in the distance reveals the locality of an Indian canoe. Sometimes there is smoke on the shore. Sometimes an Indian trader returns with the avails of his winter's traffic. A gathering storm or threatening wind arises. All at once the voyageurs burst out into one of their simple and melodious boat-songs, and the gazing at the vastness is relieved and sympathy at once awakened in gayety. Such are the scenes that attend the navigation of this mighty but solitary body of water. That nature has created such a scene of magnificence merely to look at, is contrary to her usual economy. The sources of a busy future commerce lie concealed, and but half concealed, in its rocks. Its depths abound in fish, which will be eagerly sought, and even its forests are not without timber to swell the objects of a future commerce.

Explorer Henry Schoolcraft, circa 1855, was "amazed and delighted" by the magnitude of Lake Superior. *Photo by Beal Brothers, Minnesota Historical Society*

By 1835, the small sails unfurled from missionaries' canoes had given way to hundred-ton wooden schooners, such as the one German-born John Jacob Astor named after himself. Considered America's first millionaire as organizer of the American Fur Company, Astor and his boat opened modern navigation on Lake Superior. As the abundance of furs became depleted in the 1830s, Astor diversified into commercial fishing, hauling five thousand barrels a year back east. And the North West Company's many trading posts along the lakeshores merged with the Hudson's Bay Company, pushing into the high profits of Canada's north woods.

By the 1840s, the fur trade was tapped out and the trading posts abandoned. After two hundred years of trade between the Cree, Dakota, Ojibwe, and Assiniboine on one side and the French, British, and Americans on the other, business activity fell dormant in what was about to become northern Minnesota.

An 1854 treaty passed the Minnesota coastline of Lake Superior from Ojibwe to U.S. control, accelerating a buzz among copper and gold prospectors. In the days before the LaPointe Treaty was signed, speculators sneaked up the North Shore to try to stop each other from staking premature claims.

Across the lake at Sault Sainte Marie, the Hudson's Bay Company had built a small lock and sluice in the 1790s. With small traces of copper showing up in nearby streams, the push intensified to open

Two men overlook the Duluth piers in 1885. Minneapolis Journal *photo courtesy of the* Minneapolis Star Tribune *library*

the Soo Locks to bigger boats. And on June 18, 1855, despite a cholera epidemic and brutal work, a million-dollar Soo Canal opened the area as never before.

Back across the lake, Duluth was born in 1856, but growth didn't erupt until 1869, when construction began on the Lake Superior & Mississippi Railroad. The fourteen families populating Duluth in January 1869 mushroomed to 3,500 people by year's end. Swedes, Norwegians, and Finns swarmed up the waterfront hillsides, as did sawmills, warehouses, and grain elevators. Steamboats made regular trips to Duluth from Chicago, Detroit, and Buffalo, some 1,200 miles down the lake highway.

As the 1800s came to a close, the North Shore remained an isolated wilderness, reachable only by steamers. The North Shore Highway of Route 61 wouldn't connect the region to Duluth until 1926.

A rich Philadelphia financier named Charlemagne Tower took up a Duluth banker's pitch to invest in mineral rights near Lake Vermilion in 1875. An iron outcrop where the Soudan Mine would later descend had caused a brief stir in 1865, but Tower shrugged off the Mesabi's lean findings and focused his resources on the Vermilion ore samples boasting nearly 70 percent iron content.

Steel companies, having churned through Wisconsin and Michigan iron ore supplies, demanded more. Prices jumped from $5 per ton to

$9 per ton between 1878 and 1880, just as Tower was purchasing

twenty thousand acres of Iron Range. Legislators down in St. Paul

pitched in, creating a royalty of a penny per shipped ton, which added

up to a windfall for Tower and his cohorts. Tower used the new prof-

its to land the charter of the Duluth & Iron Railway, which would

run between the ore fields and Lake Superior.

An unknown artist's sketch shows Duluth in 1882, ten years after
a canal was dug to let fishing boats through Minnesota Point. Duluth's
population grew from 3,000 in 1880 to 33,000 in 1890. *Courtesy of
the* Minneapolis Star Tribune *library*

Philadelphia financier Charlemagne Tower was among the first to invest in the mineral rights on Minnesota's Iron Range, where the town of Tower bears his name. *Minnesota Historical Society*

Wooden docks five hundred feet tall popped up in Two Harbors by 1885, allowing trains to dump ore into ships. Five hundred miners, mostly immigrants from different countries, soon worked at the Soudan Mine outside the town named after Tower. Comprised of three-man teams of immigrants who spoke varying languages, labor union organizing was slowed.

A couple of brothers in Cleveland, George and Sam Ely, purchased the first cargo of Minnesota ore: 2,818 tons shipped by train on the first of August 1884. The cargo was loaded onto the steamer *Hecla* and a barge tied along in consort named the *Ironton*.

It didn't take long for the fat cats to take notice. The Carnegies of Cleveland started buying hundreds of thousands of tons of ore at a time. A syndicate of financial giants, including Standard Oil tycoons John D. and William Rockefeller and Chicago merchant Marshall Field, soon elbowed onto Tower's turf. In 1886, Tower sold his interests to the group for a cool $8.5 million, at the time the largest cash transaction ever recorded.

Seven brothers of the Merritt family of Duluth came across the first soft ore of the Mesabi Range in 1890, near what's now known as Mountain Iron, Minnesota. In a speech forty years later, Lewis Merritt recalled "just how beautiful that ore was, glinting blue there under the deep green of the pines."

In 1888, for the first time, iron ore became the dominant trade on the Great Lakes, eclipsing coal, lumber, and grain, which had all replaced each other as the top products of earlier eras.

As more mines clawed away at the forests, loading advancements reduced the need for dozens of dock workers to move the ore from the trains to the boats. George Hulett's new unloader debuted in Conneaut, Ohio, in 1899 and made it possible to move a thousand tons an hour with barely a dockhand involved. In a few short decades, the fifty-cent-per-ton cost of unloading vessels by wheelbarrow dropped to a nickel per ton by 1900—thanks to the new technology.

Banker J. P. Morgan bought out the Carnegies' holdings for $492 million and gobbled up the Rockefellers' mining, shipping, and rail interests for $8.5 million in cash and $80 million in stock. The 1901 merger—folding together eight steel and mining companies, seventy-eight blast furnaces, hundreds of miles of railroad tracks, and vast holdings of coal and iron ore—created a monster known as United States Steel. Among the Steel Trust's most prized assets was an armada of 112 Great Lakes freighters. All told, the gigantic company produced seven million tons of steel annually—some 60 percent of the nation's steel industry—at the dawn of the twentieth century when the country was poised to build skyscrapers, automobiles, bridges, and war machines.

The Merritt brothers of Duluth discovered the first soft ore of the Mesabi Range in 1890, which Lewis (*second from the left, top row*) recalled as "glinting blue there under the deep green of the pines." *Minnesota Historical Society*

Minnesota helped power that engine of progress, with its ore production vaulting nearly fivefold from 43 million tons in the 1890s to 209 million tons in the first decade of the 1900s.

III

"From the birch bark canoe and the batteau to
vessels that hold in their bowels the farm products
of a county, the change has been accomplished
within the life period of an aged man."

~ *History of St. Louis County,* 1910

In the three hundred–plus years since the white man turned the Lakes into a commercial corridor, the products evolved from beaver pelts satisfying fashion cravings to grain and lumber and ore that fed and built a booming nation. The boats evolved as well, from birch bark canoes and flat-bottomed batteaux that hoisted tarp-sized sails to gigantic steel-hulled floating factories more than seven hundred feet long.

One thing tied the three centuries of lake shipping together: shipwrecks.

The very first commercial vessel on the Great Lakes foundered in September 1679. A French explorer named Rene-Robert Cavalier, Sieur de LaSalle, insisted that he was destined to discover a water route through New France to the Orient. He believed that route weaved through the Great Lakes.

LaSalle's crew portaged around Niagara Falls and began construction of a twin-masted, fifty-ton smaller replica of the vessel that had sailed them across the Atlantic Ocean. At the mouth of a creek near Buffalo, in the face of heated objection from the local Iroquois, shipwrights worked through the winter with heavy timber filled with frozen sap. There was no time to age the wood as Old World custom dictated. This was the New World, and with it came a new sense of urgency.

Bearing a carved eagle perched high on the stern and a jig-boom, LaSalle's boat took its name from the mythical beast chiseled into its bow.

The *Griffon*, with the head and wings of an eagle and the body of a lion, crossed Lake Erie and entered the Detroit River on August 11, 1679. Father Louis Hennepin, a Jesuit missionary making the trek, was captivated by the "vast prairies, extending back to hills covered with vines, fruit trees, thickets and tall forest trees, so disturbed as to seem rather the work of art than nature."

The *Griffon* sailed northward through Lake Huron to Lake Michigan and present-day Green Bay. That's where LaSalle decided to push on in his own canoe and send the *Griffon* back to Niagara Falls with a $12,000 payload of beaver pelts collected by missionaries and traders. Father Hennepin and the others bristled at the change of plans.

"Contrary to our opinion," Hennepin wrote, "the Sieur de la Salle who never took anyone's advice, resolved to send back his bark . . . and all the peltries . . . with a clerk and five good sailors."

They were told to unload the furs at Niagara Falls and return fully stocked with supplies. They left on September 18, 1679, "with a very favorable light west wind," Hennepin recalled, "making their adieu by firing a single cannon."

The white sails soon vanished over the horizon and the *Griffon* was never seen again. Some blamed local tribes. Others speculated that a mutiny had gone down. But Indians told Hennepin they'd seen "the bark tossing in an extraordinary manner, unable to resist the tempest . . . so that she foundered."

Nearly three hundred years later, Captain Ernest McSorley made what some speculated would be his last trip before retirement, hauling 26,116 tons of taconite pellets from Lake Superior to the steel mills of Detroit. The *Edmund Fitzgerald* pushed off on a warm, Indian summer day on November 10, 1975. But, as is common during November's last runs, Lake Superior soon whipped up in a gale.

"It's the worst sea I've ever been in," McSorley hollered into his radio during one of his final transmissions, some seventeen miles off Whitefish Point, Caribou Island, and the Six Fathoms Shoal. On glassy days, the reef hid thirty-six feet below Lake Superior's surface. The *Edmund Fitzgerald* sat thirty feet deep, and the wind had stirred the waves up to thirty-five-feet high.

Some later testified that Captain McSorley was preoccupied with his wife's failing health. They said he rarely anchored for bad weather. Others contended he left hatches untended to avoid overtime pay.

"We're holding our own," were his last words over the radio.

McSorley and his crew of twenty-eight remain onboard the *Edmund Fitzgerald* in an underwater tomb, where diving is now prohibited.

Between the *Griffon* and the *Edmund Fitzgerald*, at least 1,077 storm-related shipwrecks now litter the Lake bottoms. With early recordkeeping somewhat sketchy, that number has been estimated to reach more than six thousand.

More than fifty great storms have been recorded on the Great Lakes since 1835. And at least one ship was lost for eighty-five consecutive seasons, between 1846 and 1930. In the early 1900s, things were particularly dangerous, with twenty-five losses in 1901, twenty-two in 1902, and thirty-four in 1903.

The number of shipwrecks nearly doubled by the end of the 1905 shipping season.

One third of all theses wrecks have come in November, when bitter air swings down from Hudson Bay and the Arctic above while warm air can still be blowing up from the Western plains.

Air masses packing sharply different temperatures collide, sparking a counterclockwise eastward twist in the atmosphere and triggering violent storms. When the massive weather systems move out over the warmer, moist Great Lakes, everything intensifies.

IV

"We shall be very pleased if November turns out to be milder than usual. The month will show up strong in the ore shipping column for the season if conditions are favorable. The impression prevails that we shall have a late season, and that would be welcomed by shipping interests."

~ Pittsburgh Steamship Company executive
Allyn Harvey, November 7, 1905

Ice, fog, fire, and death punctuated the start of the 1905 shipping season. By season's end, the total tonnage of freight crisscrossing Lake Superior would leap 40 percent over 1904 figures. But the precursors of dread started in April and didn't let up until after Thanksgiving.

Seven steel-hulled ships left Duluth on April 10 to pick up tons of ore twenty-five miles up the North Shore in Two Harbors. Among these ships were the *Mataafa* and the *Crescent City*, part of the Pittsburgh Steamship Company's massive 112-vessel armada. When they reached the eastern end of Lake Superior, they joined twenty other boats locked in a windblown ice field extending out six miles in the bay at Whitefish Point.

"There are now twenty-two steamers imprisoned in the ice, some of which have been icebound for ten days," the *Duluth Evening Herald* reported.

An ice breaker was dispatched. Crewmembers were forced to hike across the ice to replenish dwindling supplies. And more than a dozen boats wound up ramming each other once freed from the frozen lake water.

Most of the ships were made of steel, newer and longer floating boxes carrying more and more ore with now underpowered engines. Some wooden steamers still sailed Lake Superior, but that shrinking fleet was clearly heading toward extinction. One of the wooden boats, the 250-foot *Hesper*, was stunned when a spring nor'easter blew up on May 3. Its sixty-mile-per-hour winds felt more like November and pushed the *Hesper* to the southern edge of Silver Bay Harbor up the North Shore.

The crew made it to safety on two lifeboats, but the steamer was ripped apart. Its smokestack toppled and cabins tossed off the side, the *Hesper* lay in debris scattered for five miles. And eyebrows shot up when it was revealed that the boat, worth all of $80,000, had just been insured for $50,000 weeks earlier. The captain and crew refused to talk to reporters. Insurance rates had skyrocketed to $20,000 for the new $300,000 boats. Big companies, like Pittsburgh Steamship, refused to pay the hefty premiums and took their chances uninsured.

Fog in May prompted a collision of another wooden boat, the *William P. Rend*, into the eastern side of Manitou Island off the pointing finger of Keweenaw Peninsula that juts up from Superior's southern shore. (Three years earlier, under its previous name, the *George G. Hadley*, the ship had crashed into the whaleback steamer *Thomas Wilson* off the Duluth piers, killing nine.)

The troublesome 1905 shipping season turned deadly on the first of September. Duluth weather forecaster Herbert Richardson posted storm flags. Captains ignored them. They didn't worry about the weather with November still a couple months away.

By September 3, watchman John Lindquist of the whaleback steamer *Samuel Mather* had been swept overboard and drowned off Knife Island near Duluth. Near Outer Island in the Apostle Islands, the 372-foot steamer *Sevona* raked over a reef, gashing a widening crack by hatch No. 4. The sixteen men in the stern rowed lifeboats to shore. But Captain D. S. MacDonald and six crewmembers in the forepeak drowned when they tried their luck on life rafts, which splintered beneath them in the waves. Lumberjacks and homesteaders aided the survivors, but three Bayfield men were arrested for robbing the bodies of the dead.

In the same early September tempest, five of the ten sailors aboard drowned off Outer Island when the *Pretoria's* lifeboat capsized.

Lighthouse keeper John Irvine provided the five survivors with warm soup and blankets.

The worst death toll from the September storm involved the wooden steamer *Iosco* and the barge she towed, *Olive Jeanette*. They left Duluth laden with ore on August 30 and made it to Keweenaw Point. Fifteen bodies, wearing cork-filled life preservers and no shoes, washed up on nearby beaches. A sixteenth body turned up the next summer.

A homesteader found a pair of underwear bearing the initials "N. G." in the woods. Someone had apparently dragged *Iosco* captain Nelson Gonyaw's body off the beach, stolen the $800 he typically carried, and buried him in the forest. His brother came from Michigan to search for the body, but the captain's grave was never found.

Two weeks later, fire erupted on the wooden steamer *V. H. Ketchum*, and the lifeboat flipped in 23 feet of water off Parisienne Island on the Canadian side of Whitefish Point. Mate Andrew Johnson swam after Mrs. B. Ames, the boat's cook, and both drowned in the struggle.

The 1905 season up to this point had been marked with tragedy, but business was robust. Despite the disasters and deaths, a profitable finish loomed on the horizon. All that was needed was a strong November that could sew up the 1905 shipping season with a flourish.

PART 2

Storm Within the Storm

I

"November is the archfiend, who in his glowering, dismal thirty days is certain to be harboring with his own horrid mockery a northeast gale."

~ Mary Ellen Chase (1887–1973)

"Dear Son: . . . There has been more stormy weather, but I have dared to presume that you are safe and sound. . . ."

~ Letter from Toronto fruit merchant
H. W. Woodgate to his son,
Thomas, a coal-shoveling fireman
on Great Lakes freighters
November 17, 1905

Boats line the Mesabi Ore Dock in Duluth around 1905. *Courtesy of the Minneapolis Star Tribune library*

Duluth's docks buzzed with clattering horses' hooves and the booming sound of red-rock iron tumbling from tipped train cars into steel-hulled freighters. A fine red powder—ore dust—covered cargo, wagons, and ropes.

It was just about noon on Monday, November 27, 1905. Thanksgiving was coming. Some boats were already heading for winter layup. But for most, the final rush of the shipping season was underway. At last.

Captains made last-minute hires. Stevedores loaded cargo onto boats small and large. Most of the old wooden schooners had been replaced. Sails were rare sights. Massive bulk freighters crowded the harbor. Like floating factories, the boats resembled gigantic shoeboxes with a point in the front and a propeller aft. Their smokestacks spewed black smoke, engines firing, for one last run down the thousand-mile watery highway, across the Great Lakes, down to Lake Erie and the steel mills of Ohio and Pennsylvania.

Sailors with canvas sea bags hoisted on their shoulders tiptoed over thick, snaking ropes and between big-wheeled carts. Everyone was antsy. One week earlier, the captains had heeded the red storm flags and waited out the three-day blow that had whipped Lake Superior like a witch's cauldron.

From newspapers, gossip, and a few firsthand accounts, word of the storm's sixty-mile-per-hour gusts and sheets of slushy snow had filtered back to Bill Lanigan's pub on Superior Street. That's where the sailors and captains and newspaper folk spent the end of last week. Among the members of the press in Duluth in 1905 was a spunky woman named Mary McFadden, the city's first full-time newspaperwoman. A natural storyteller herself, McFadden loved nothing more than listening to the captains' tales.

One boat, a little 250-foot wooden steamer named after one of the ore trade's giants, the *Charlemagne Tower Jr.*, had sailed out of Duluth that past Thursday, downbound with a load of iron ore. The storm flattened the wooden cabin on the rear of boat. When the steamer hobbled into Keweenaw Waterway on Lake Superior's jutting southern peninsula, the captain vowed to reporters that he would never again be out on Lake Superior when he should be in port. That gave the men at Lanigan's a laugh. And the woman, Mary McFadden.

McFadden's soft chin, hook nose, dark eyes, and pulled-back hair gave off a no-nonsense air. She was plenty tough, covering the docks, the boats, the lumbermen, and the ore trade of Duluth. Mary McFadden was twenty-nine and blossoming into a popular editorial writer. She was drawn to the human drama of the Inland Seas and covered the storms with a special flare.

McFadden was the oldest of a dozen siblings. Her mother, Julia, died birthing her thirteenth baby in tiny Graceville, on Minnesota's western edge. McFadden was seventeen when her mother died. She tried to take over mothering the young ones. But her spirit was restless. And her love for writing prevailed. She headed off to the University of Minnesota and wound up working at the *Minneapolis Times*. She moved up to Duluth in 1903, drawn to the bustle, the commerce, and, most of all, the giant Lake Superior.

McFadden wrote up the story of the little wooden steamer, the *Charlemagne Tower Jr.* She loved to interview the masters of the Great Lakes vessels. They frustrated her with their quiet ways, seldom boasting or exaggerating. She begged them to open up and share their emotions. They shrugged and said it was their job, that's all.

After the sixty-mile-per-hour winds had finally blown themselves out that Friday, the weekend brought fair weather. And now it was time to get back on the Lakes for one last dash before a relaxing winter with wives and parents and children.

Most of the men crisscrossing the dock were built like bears from a long season of shoveling coal and working the boats. They worked straight through. There was no time to go home, no time to rest. Profits in a short season depended on nonstop loading and unloading and ships coming and going constantly. Unlike ocean seamen, though, Great Lakes sailors could almost always see land. Wives cradling babies would wave at the blast of the boat whistle and squint to see their men. Even when the boats sailed far from lakefront towns and cities, past forests and islands and through the thick smell of pine, vessel men on the Inland Seas could usually see other boats in the crowded shipping lanes. They often towed barges behind them to enhance profits.

Some of the men on the Duluth docks that noon were Canadians. Others were Englishmen and Scandinavian, with trumpeting accents. Plenty were American born and raised.

And there were black men on the docks, as well: cook Walter Bush, steward Henry Wright, and porter Fred Saunders from Amherstburg, Ontario, had hired on when the massive, 430-foot-long *Mataafa* stopped in their port. Two pieces of paper were tucked in Henry Wright's pocket: membership card No. 121 of the Marine Cooks and Stewards' Union and a signed receipt showing he'd paid his dues for December 1905. Wright was among two dozen weary sailing men squeezing out some last wages before winter, preparing the *Mataafa* for one last ore-hauling trip to the ports of Lake Erie and the steel foundries of Ohio and Pennsylvania.

James Early, one of the *Mataafa's* assistant engineers, couldn't wait to get back to Buffalo. As the crew waited out the three-day storm in Duluth, Early had received a telegram from his new bride. They were married the year before in 1904. The telegram told Early that he had become the father of a tiny daughter. One more run and he'd be able to hold his new baby and breathe in her sweet smell.

Many of the vessel men on the dock were catching on with new boats, which offered a little more money to carry them over the winter. Thomas Woodgate, for one, had been shoveling coal in the firehold of the *Kensington*, a Great Lakes freighter sailing out of Michigan. A week earlier, Woodgate had shipped upon the *Mataafa* in Conneaut, Ohio. *Mataafa* Captain Richard Humble, himself from Conneaut, couldn't help but be impressed with Woodgate's chiseled, Herculean build, forged from a season shoveling coal in sweaty boiler rooms.

Woodgate carried three twenty-dollar bills in a note case and a bank deposit slip showing that he had put away fifty dollars in the First National Bank in Erie, Pennsylvania, earlier in November. He also carried a folded letter in his pocket. He had received it nine days earlier, when he jumped the *Kensington* and hired on to the *Mataafa*. The letter, from his father's fruit-selling office in Toronto, said:

Dear Son:

Your letter came to hand, for which I thank you and it always gives pleasure to hear from you. I am glad you are well. There has been more stormy weather, but as it would take all the U.S. Navy to wreck the old "Kensington," I have dared to presume that you are safe and sound. I now say bye bye as I hope soon to see you. I am exercising patience until the time arrives and you reach the port.

With much love from your affectionate father,

H. W. Woodgate

Toronto, Ont., Nov. 17, 2005

II

"Captain Thomas Honner is one of the ablest officers
on the Great Lakes and . . . his reputation as a safe
and reliable captain was by this time well-established."

~ _History of the Great Lakes_, 1899

While most of the men pushing past each other on the Duluth docks were young, plenty of old-timers were around as well. At fifty-eight, Thomas Honner had tried to retire a couple of times. After a long career that included many an ocean voyage, he'd been certified as a hull inspector. It was a safe civil service job, but it made him restless. He'd mastered a tugboat in Detroit for a while. And he'd spent most of the 1905 season commanding a steamer on Lake Michigan, running between Chicago and his home in Grand Haven, Michigan.

Eleven years earlier Honner had married a Chicago girl, Elizabeth Duffy, up Lake Michigan in Kenosha, Wisconsin. She had already produced three adorable children: Thomas, Doris, and little Bennie. After completing the 1905 season on the _City of the Straits_, Honner had returned to his cozy home in Grand Haven. But the itch of the Inland Seas got to him.

And when the captain of the _Ira H. Owen_ grew ill, Honner agreed to sign on as first mate and command the 262-foot, double-stacked steamer. The boat was eighteen years old but appeared staunch and seaworthy. While he waited out the storm in Duluth, Honner ordered an overhaul of the hatch fastenings.

So when his stevedores loaded the *Owen* with 116,500 bushels of barley that Monday morning, Honner felt as confident as he'd ever been this late in the season. Compared to the tonnage of the ore boats surrounding his vessel, Honner was hauling a light load. But he figured that would keep the boat high in the water.

Honner, the ailing captain Joseph Hulligan, and their crew of seventeen chugged out of the Duluth Ship Canal about noon. The ship was headed east across Lake Superior, down through the lower Lakes to Buffalo and eventually back to Grand Haven and the warm embrace of Elizabeth Honner and the three young ones.

A few hours later, about 3:30 p.m., a boat twice as large, the *Mataafa*, sluggishly inched through the chutes formed by the canal's two-thousand-foot stone piers. As was common, the *Mataafa* towed a barge. Newer ships coming out of the yards, six-hundred-footers, were making the old practice of barge-towing obsolete. For now, though, towing two loads of ore under the power of one engine simply made a cheap form of shipping that much cheaper. Whether transporting red iron ore, lumber, or barley, moving freight by boat cost half the price of moving it by railroad. And return loads of coal added to the profits.

Captain Thomas Honner agreed to commandeer the twin-stacker
Ira H. Owen at the last minute, when the ship's customary captain
fell ill. *Courtesy of Tom Honore of Woolwine, Virginia, his grandson*

Dick Humble stood in the *Mataafa*'s white pilot house. At thirty-two years old, his boyish looks masked more than a dozen years of experience. A dozen Novembers. He sailed right beneath the storm flags that Monday afternoon. He always relied on his judgment over the weather bureau or the bigwigs down in Cleveland. That's why he'd waited out the last storm. But now, custom and his gut agreed: A few calm days invariably followed rough seas. Lolling around Duluth's port any longer was senseless.

The wind, out of the northeast, felt fresh. The waves that kissed the *Mataafa*'s steel hull were more gentle than menacing.

III

"Wind storms occur occasionally but their strength
and frequency compare favorably with other sections
of the country and tornadoes are an unknown feature
in this locality."
~ Duluth weather forecaster Herbert Richardson, 1914

Herbert Richardson felt as antsy as the sailors and the captains down on the docks. Like the freighter captains, Richardson found himself in the midst of a conundrum that Monday, November 27, 1905. He, too, was torn between staying and going, although he wouldn't be heading out on Lake Superior. The Ionic Lodge No. 186 was calling him, as it did every second and fourth Monday for meeting nights. All of Duluth's business and community leaders gathered in the lodge. The camaraderie, the civic goals, and the laughter captivated Richardson almost as much as his job.

As the U.S. Weather Bureau forecaster in Duluth, Richardson felt compelled to monitor the readings from his rooftop gauges, vanes, and anemometer cups. In his first-floor study, he wound the clock-work mechanisms that made the pens dance on his graph paper, recording barometric pressures and dropping temperatures.

His morning regional weather map, telegraphed from Washington, foretold a coming clash. Cold weather was dropping down from the Arctic and a warmer, humid system was sailing up from the southwest. When they collided, Richardson knew, the battleground would likely be the gray slate of Lake Superior that stretched out before him.

He had ordered northeast storm signals hoisted. But the daytime warnings and the red-and-white lanterns that provided nighttime alerts had been up so often lately, Richardson feared the captains would take them for granted. They never had much trust in his forecasts, the cocky masters. That's why he had been proud when last week's storm, packing sixty-mile-per-hour gusts and slushy snow, hadn't cost any lives. The captains had stayed in port just as Herbert suggested.

Duluth weather forecaster Herbert Richardson records weather data in his house and weather station, which he built in 1904. *National Oceanic and Atmospheric Administration and National Weather Service archives*

But at noon, he shook his head and watched the little twin stacker *Ira Owen* ease out of the canal. By 3:30 in the afternoon, he could see the larger *Mataafa* sailing out of the canal and into the gray skies. And he couldn't really blame them. The weekend had been quiet. It had been a crummy season, with more than the usual number of storms in September and October. And more mishaps, too. He knew the bosses at U.S. Steel wanted their massive Pittsburgh Steamship fleet, which included the *Mataafa* among its 112 boats, to make one final run across the Lakes. The bottom line depended on it.

Richardson double-checked all the recording equipment, making sure there was enough paper and enough ink and that everything was well wound for the evening. He tugged on the vest of his woolen three-piece suit and straightened his tie. He combed his cottony hair along its part above his left eye and ran the comb through his well-trimmed mustache. The weather data could wait. This was a day he had been anticipating for years.

At thirty-eight, he would become one of the youngest city fathers to have the third degree conferred, promoting him to the rank of Master Mason at Ionic Lodge No. 186. The old Masonic Lodge stood on the corner of Second and East Superior streets. The lodge was a seven-story stone building with an onion dome perched ornately on the rooftop. It had served the masons well since 1880 but was in its final days. They would move into new quarters the next spring. But tonight, more than two hundred of Duluth's most prominent men would gather to honor Richardson during a lavish dinner meeting at six o'clock.

As he prepared to trudge down the hill to the temple, Richardson paused and surveyed the dark-varnished walls of his first-floor office, the weather maps, telegraph and telephone stations, and gas lamps that illuminated his spinning, whirling climatology gadgets. He had to leave. But first, he'd check the gauges on the roof.

He climbed the wooden steps and heard his twelve-year-old son, James, upstairs with Dorothy, Richardson's wife, no doubt reviewing the story of the Pilgrims for his schoolwork. Thanksgiving was almost upon them. He hoped the story resonated with Jimmy. After all, his forebears had been Pilgrims themselves back in the 1620s.

Snow was falling as Richardson stepped on the rooftop about five o'clock and placed his hands on the freshly painted white balustrade railing. A whisper of daylight remained and reflected on Lake Superior below him. Gas streetlamps lent the city a glow, the snow flickering wet and thick. The smell of coal smoke and ethnic cooking swirled in the chilled breeze.

Duluth had grown so much in Richardson's seven years as the city's weather forecaster. The latest count put the population at 64,945, up 13,000 from the turn-of-the-century census. The city boasted 406 teachers and 345 bartenders and liquor sellers. There were 1,800 men in the lumber business and 1,700 working the railroads. The largest segment of the workers, nearly 9,000 men, were considered common laborers. They came to Duluth to build the new tall brick office towers that climbed up the horseshoe hillside surrounding the busy, three-hundred-acre harbor.

Herbert Richardson had felt a gush of pride when he read that Duluth had eclipsed London as the world's second busiest port, trailing only New York harbor. All those tons of ore, lumber, and grain moved out of Duluth in a short eight-month season at a rate five times higher than year-round ports near the Panama or Suez canals. On an average day, Richardson could see fifty boats, one every thirty minutes, come and go through the two-thousand-foot-long stone piers that defined the Duluth Ship Canal.

One year earlier, in 1904, Richardson had designed every inch of his eleven-room house. The handsome, blond-brick home stood square as a jewelry box and symmetrical in the way of government structures. Yet the white wooden shutters and smartly railed porch gave it a touch of homeyness. He couldn't have picked a better spot for the new headquarters of the U.S. Weather Bureau. The lot was large, allowing ample room to mount rain and snow gauges on a cement platform thirty feet from the house. He'd dug the troughs for the lead-covered underground cables, which he connected to the registering apparatus in the office downstairs.

The thermometer station was fifty feet behind the house, with each thermometer ten feet above ground. The rooftop instruments— the sunshine recorder, wind vane, and anemometer cups—stood forty-eight feet above ground. Richardson had carefully measured the distances, the way he carefully measured everything. He enjoyed telling visitors that the house stood 532 feet above Lake Superior and 1,133 feet above sea level. The basement windows, if anyone asked, were 525 feet above the lake.

Duluth's Masonic Lodge is where Herbert Richardson was honored the night the storm broke on November 27, 1905. *Photo by Charles P. Gibson, Minnesota Historical Society*

Duluth's Incline rail line, pictured in 1908, faintly shows meteorologist Herbert Richardson's home and station on the hilltop. *Courtesy of the Minneapolis Star Tribune library*

The Seventh Avenue Incline Railway stopped at a hilltop station nearby. Facing southeast from his bench-like plateau, Richardson could see the entire city and Duluth's companion port of Superior, Wisconsin.

He could see the new aerial lift bridge that spanned the twin stone piers jutting out to form the canal. He could make out the eight-foot red storm flags he had ordered hoisted earlier that day when his Washington telegraph revealed that snow was falling thick across the wind-whipped North Dakota plains.

From his rooftop, Richardson gazed through the fading light. He could barely make out the web of railroad tracks converging on the ore docks, where train cars dumped red-rock iron into the hatches of the long, steel-hulled ships. A crew of stevedores began unloading cargo from a steel freighter he recognized as the *S. C. Reynolds*. Richardson wondered for an instant why the hands had tied the boat way out on the end of the city dock, far from the safety closer to shore. Even the dockhands had ignored his storm flags.

If he squinted hard, he could see the streetlamps outside Lanigan's pub on Superior Street, where the captains and sailors loved to swap tales. He could see the boarding houses and brothels.

Mostly, though, Richardson looked out at the water. The waves were starting to build. But it was time to go. When he returned home, he would be a Grand Master. And the wind would be blowing with an icy bitterness Richardson would never forget. By seven o'clock that night, while he sat in the warm Mason Lodge, surrounded by Duluth's elite, the wind gauges back at his home office on the hill were registering 44 miles per hour. Within a half-hour, the storm would explode.

IV

"I have sailed the Great Lakes for the last ten years,

but never have I been in so desperate a position nor

seen so terrible a storm."

~ *Crescent City* wheelman Charlie Abrams

While the *Ira Owen* and *Mataafa* plodded slowly up Lake Superior's western bay and into the largest freshwater basin on the planet, another line of boats headed west. They'd waited out the storm and sat around all that Saturday at the Soo Locks of Sault Sainte Marie, where Michigan and Canada meet. The locks form the faucet at the eastern edge of Lake Superior.

When the sun climbed Sunday into clear skies and the huge doors of the lock opened, the *Crescent City* spilled out on its 350-mile trek across Lake Superior. The 406-foot boat was heading to fill its empty hold with ore in Two Harbors, Minnesota, some twenty-five miles north of Duluth, before circling back to Ashtabula and winter layup in Ohio. The *William Edenborn*, towing a barge named *Madeira*, cleared the Soo Locks about the same time.

Arthur Daggett, his hair disheveled above a pug nose, wiry mustache, and jutting jaw, stood at the watch on the bow of the *Crescent City*. He was glad the ride across Superior had been uneventful that

Sunday night and most of Monday. As he pulled up his coat collar and stared out over a darkening Lake Superior that Monday evening, Daggett's mind wandered backward. As a boy growing up in Collingwood, Ontario, he had always loved the water. He quickly grew into a strong swimmer. His hometown sat far across the Great Lakes in a sheltered cove of Lake Huron's Nottawasaga Bay. That's clear across Superior, four hundred miles east of Duluth and a couple hundred miles overland from Toronto.

The Lakes, though, had really been Daggett's home. He was one of a mushrooming cadre of Great Lakes sailing men, manning freighters to cheaply move ore, farm goods, and lumber across the water to the Pittsburgh steel foundries and the industrial maws of Buffalo, Cleveland, Sandusky, and Ashtabula. Daggett was one of the vessel hands who made bulk freighters such a handy economical tool. Like many who worked the boats, he had plenty of pluck, too.

Only twenty-eight years old, Daggett had seen more drama on the Lakes than some old-timers witness in a lifetime. In 1897, a wooden schooner sank below him on Lake Michigan. He was able to tread water long enough for a lifeboat to scoop him up. Five years later, Daggett was sleeping aboard the *Wilson*, a whaleback steamer laden with ore, when he was jarred awake. When the *George G. Hadley* swung right for the port in Superior, it rammed into the downbound *Wilson*, and the collision ignited a fire. The crash woke Daggett, and he jumped just as the stern arched into the air. A cook named Tripp jumped with him. Tripp had grown up with Daggett on the protected bay of Collingwood. But he wasn't quite the swimmer Daggett was.

Daggett twice dropped below Lake Superior's chilly surface. When he fought his way back up to the air, he saw Tripp frantically treading water. The third time they went down, Daggett came up alone, gulping for air. He swam toward the *Hadley* and was rescued by a tugboat and ferried to Duluth. Nine of Daggett's shipmates drowned after the boat sank in seventy-five feet of water just beyond Duluth's view. Tripp was never seen again. Lake Superior did not give up his body.

Daggett's memories grew more haunted as the waves below him steadily began to climb. They were almost to the western edge of Lake Superior and the rocky cliffs of Minnesota's forested North Shore. The wind really started to puff by eight o'clock that Monday night. With it, the waves grew tall and choppy.

Daggett peered out from the watch above the bow, into the darkness that began to envelop Lake Superior. Snowflakes danced in the gusts before him as the *Crescent City* crept through the rolling troughs. Daggett watched for the lighthouses on Keweenaw Point and Caribou, Gull Rock, Manitou, and Outer islands.

Elsewhere on the *Crescent City*, Daggett's shipmates leaned into their work with an empty feeling in their stomachs. There had been no time for supper and no appetite for it either. Hattie Stevens, the cook's wife, had brought a couple turkeys along for the crew's Thanksgiving dinner, but that was several days away.

Engineer A. E. Buddemeyer, who hailed from Grand Rapids, Michigan, stood in the hot, encased engine room, manning the levers and shafts of the pounding, triple-expansion steam engine. Standing at the controls, Buddemeyer looked like an orchestra conductor, shutting down the engine when the stern rose out of the water, then re-engaging the power when the wave had been hurdled.

In the adjacent boiler room, men staggered to keep their balance and shovel coal to get the ship going full tilt. They swung rhythmically in the firehold, shovel after shovel, wheelbarrow after wheelbarrow, their minds and biceps numb in the hot darkness. Velvety black smoke oozed out of the silver smokestack, which was ringed at the top with black paint and soot.

First Mate James Thomson of Buffalo kept his eye on the glass, knowing a high barometer reading this late in the season spelled trouble. He told Captain Frank Rice when it started dropping like a stone. Rice ordered the engine room to give all the power it could. He called for his wheelman to turn the ship starboard and port, but the wind was becoming too strong for such maneuvering. The *Crescent City* was losing its bearings.

As midnight that Monday approached, Rice deemed Two Harbors

too difficult to navigate and headed down the coast toward Duluth. They would try to hang on for thirty more miles and make it to Duluth's harbor and, eventually, Lanigan's pub, where Rice looked forward to trading tales of the wicked gale with other captains. He wondered if any could remember a storm coming so quickly on the heels of an earlier blow.

A mate dropped a sounding lead over the side and hollered to the captain that the depth was no more than one hundred feet. The coast was drawing closer. About one o'clock in the morning of Tuesday, November 28, Rice hollered to drop both anchors, which clanged as their chains vanished in the black water. For three hours, the anchors steadied the ship. And the *Crescent City* inched toward Duluth.

The wind started to whip around, counterclockwise, blowing from the northwest. And it was picking up speed, gusting to sixty miles per hour. Daggett began to shiver. The temperature dropped below zero. And the *Crescent City*'s deep-throated steam whistle was blasting three short snorts per minute—the Great Lakes' signal for foggy, foul weather.

Walls of waves a dozen feet high crashed into the ship's red hull, sending spray over its smokestack. The snow fell thickly but didn't stick to the decks, blown off instead by the gusts. The *Crescent City*'s huge propeller rose out of the water, spinning in free air and forcing Buddemeyer to adjust the throttle between each valley in the combers. Waves sloshed over the ship's long deck, which quivered from stem to stern. The topside crew pulled their life belts tight, and some lashed themselves to the old spars, from which sails seldom unfurled anymore. Down below, the men worked like demons to keep the engines running at full speed.

Since midnight, Captain Rice had stood inside the white-painted pilot house up front, snug in sweaters and his great coat, as icy pellets clipped the windows. He kept his long ship pointing into the teeth of the wind, fearing a broadside turn would spell a capsize. As watchman, it was Daggett's job to scurry up to his post, ignore the risk of being swept overboard, and squint through the snow and blackness.

Ocean ships can ride out a storm for days without worrying about the rocky, craggy lakeshore that loomed just out of view. Captain Rice ordered the men to stay at their posts. A huge gust pounded the starboard bow and pulled the anchors from the lake bottom. Daggett peered through the sharp, icy snow and looked for the rocky shore. Steam covered the lake. The water was far warmer than the air.

Daggett could hear it. Above the roar of the storm, the muffled, booming, echoing sound of waves pounding cliffs. The *Crescent City* had dragged its anchors for about an hour. The shore was growing closer.

Lake Superior's North Shore took the waves that splashed against the rocky coast and flung all that energy back into the lake. Fresh water, unlike salty seas, lacks the density needed for the cresting common among curling ocean waves. Great Lakes waves are choppy and collapse abruptly. Lake Superior becomes quite a mess when you mix the chop of the waves reverberating off the shore with a crisscrossing lakescape of tall waves crumbling over each other.

Old-time sailors often told tales of the Three Sisters. When the waves bouncing back off the North Shore swept in sync with the already towering waves during a northeast gale, the Three Sisters appeared: One huge wave, followed by an even bigger monster, and then a colossal comber that doomed many of the thousand ships that now litter the deep lake bottoms.

The Minnesota coast that loomed in the darkness evoked fear and sweetness for Daggett and his mates, especially late in the season. At the moment, the shore packed more menace than the melancholy of a family waving through the glass. Daggett felt like a man sentenced to be hanged, waiting, as the sound of wave on rock gave way to the faint sight of the bluff, a dim outline on the horizon.

The captain rang the engine room and ordered the ship's engines reversed. Daggett realized his fate with a shiver. He was about to die. This wasn't like the schooner on Lake Michigan or the *Wilson*. The waves were too strong and the rocks too close to survive. This was his last hour. The rest of the crew had the same realization. They were doomed.

If it had a belly full of ore, the *Crescent City* might have a chance to weather this storm. But it was riding too high, empty except for some water in its hold for ballast.

Now, Daggett, Buddemeyer, Captain Rice, Hattie Stevens, and twenty-one others in the crew waited for the steamer to collide with the craggy coast and splinter the *Crescent City* like an eggshell. When the boat's bow crashed ashore about four in the morning, a huge wave splashed clear across the deck, throwing spray fifty feet high and drenching the crew to a tremble.

The middle of the steamer was giving way. A gash had been torn into its steel hull. Torrents of water poured into the hold. Buddemeyer and the men below scampered up to the frozen deck. Everyone gathered around Captain Rice. Daggett listened for the captain to offer a prayer for their souls.

Then Daggett noticed something odd. The boat wasn't getting pounded, sliding back into the water, and getting pounded again. Its stern had swung around after the nose smacked the rock. Somehow, the *Crescent City* had lurched broadside into a cove tucked between massive rocks fifty yards in either direction.

A cliff top could be seen through the darkness, about ten feet away. Someone quickly came forward with a rickety ladder. Timing the sway of the ship, the crew managed to rest one end of the ladder on the bank, at a downward slant from the rail.

One by one, Captain Rice called out their names and the first mate echoed his call. Mrs. Stevens went first, helped by her husband, the wheelman, and the second mate. When Daggett's name was called, he crawled through the wind's teeth, down the groaning ladder toward safety.

After the whole crew had shimmied down the ladder, Captain Rice read off all the names. When the last man muttered that, yes, he was alive and safely ashore, a feeble cheer arose. It was barely audible over the roar of the storm.

The *Crescent City*'s bow lodged on the beach one mile east of Duluth near Lakewood. *Great Lakes Marine Collection of the Milwaukee Public Library/Wisconsin Marine Historical Society*

V

"The barge would back up and then shoot against the cliff like an insane man trying to batter out his brains against a stone wall."

~ *Duluth Evening Herald,* December 1, 1905

Like many of the Great Lakes freighters, the upbound *William Edenborn* and *Madeira* sailed in consort as the wind began to blow Monday night. Both vessels were massive, more than four hundred feet long, but only the *Edenborn* had the powerful engine that slowly pushed the boats across Lake Superior. Many of the bigger engines sat at the shipyards, waiting to go into new six-hundred-footers. The new boats were built big enough that barge-towing was growing obsolete. But many tandems like this pair were out on the Lakes. The *Edenborn*, with twenty-five in its crew, plodded out of the Soo Locks that Sunday, towing behind it the *Madeira*, with a crew of nine. A giant towline linked the boats. Megaphones and ship whistles connected them less concretely. Both boats carried some water in their holds to steady them as they headed for a last load of ore in Minnesota.

As midnight that Monday approached, the snow fell in sharp, hail-like pebbles. Crewmembers could see only half the length of the boat. The snow cut into their faces. As helpless as both crews felt,

The massive barge *Madeira* had only a small motor to lower its anchors.
Historical Collections of the Great Lakes, Bowling Green State University

the men on the *Madeira* had to worry about more than the ice and the volume of waves spilling over the stern. The barge had no way to control itself, tethered to a ship it could no longer see. Its small engines only worked the anchor chains. The captains hoped to hide from the wind behind Devil's Island in the Apostle Islands, off Superior's South Shore. But the storm blew them across the water toward Minnesota's craggy North Shore instead.

Just after three o'clock that Tuesday morning, as the waves and spray and snow jostled both boats, Fred Benson and James Morrow, aboard the *Madeira*, heard a snap in the wind and felt a jolt. They both knew the towline had parted. Maybe A. J. Talbot, the *Edenborn*'s master, figured the *Madeira* was better off riding the storm out alone. Perhaps he worried about colliding in the rough seas. Or maybe a wave had snapped the line. Either way, the *Madeira* was now drifting—powerless—in the crashing water, heading toward the rocky Minnesota cliffs known as Gold Rock, and Split Rock to its south.

Morrow, the first mate, ordered the distress signal. Maybe the *Edenborn* could turn around and reconnect. Benson, a hulking Scandinavian seaman, knew the blasts were fruitless. The *Madeira* was on its own. And the snow was falling thicker now as the temperature sank and the waves grew. The barge's captain, John Dissette from Buffalo, ordered the anchors dropped. He dropped all nine hundred feet of anchor cables, hoping they would catch on the lake bottom and steady the *Madeira*. At least he hoped. No one could see in the dark snow and steam and spray of the giant waves. And the anchors, if they had dropped all the way, didn't seem to be doing anything.

For two hours, Benson, Morrow, and the other seven on the *Madeira* felt themselves drifting closer to the rocks. They could no longer worry about their peers on the *Edenborn*. They struck the shore at 5:30 Tuesday morning with a deafening thud. The bow hit first, swinging the boat broadside. They had hit smack dab into what was known as Gold Rock, a seventy-foot face of sheer rocky cliff.

Five years later, Congress would appropriate $75,000 to build Split Rock Lighthouse atop a nearby rock face. Tourists' snapshots and hand-painted postcards would make the site well known.

But when Benson and Morrow looked up in the faint morning light, they couldn't see the cliff top. And they didn't have long to gaze upward. They had to act quickly. Death was close, and the waves pounded with a rhythmic crash. As water poured over the deck, Morrow began to climb the net-like rigging of the mizzenmast. He had watched as the boat rocked with each wave and saw how close the mast swung toward the shelf atop the cliff; he would leap like an acrobat and save himself before the barge splintered to pieces. As he scooted up the mast, it arched like a willow branch between the pounding waves. Morrow soon realized his plan was futile. He could never climb high enough to cover the chasm between the top of the mast and the top of the cliff. He was glad, though, to be above the slap of the icy waves. As he lowered himself back down, a massive wave shook the *Madeira* with such force that the steel hull split in two. Morrow tumbled into the gash and was swept over the side and into the black inky water between the barge and the rocks.

That's when Benson leaped. He figured he had nothing to lose. A dozen times, the waves had smashed the *Madeira* against the cliff. The vessel wouldn't last much longer. Benson grabbed a coil of rope, fastened one end to the mast, and timed the seconds between the

The *Madeira* strikes the dark cliff known as Gold Rock, and Fred Benson makes his miraculous leap. *Artist: Kurt Carlson. Reprinted with permission of the Great Lakes Shipwreck Historical Society*

receding waves. They dropped the barge back into the water until the next towering wave would slap it against the cliff.

Benson could see a rocky shelf that might give him a foothold. What did he have to lose? When the barge groaned against Gold Rock, Benson and his coil of rope leaped and landed on a rock and grabbed an inverted tree poking out of the cliff face. He didn't hesitate; he knew that would kill him. Instead, he scaled the cliff like a spider until the first wave hit. Benson's arms and shoulders were taut and muscular. He shivered and clung to the rock as the wave washed over him. Then he shook himself from the numbing chill and scampered up the cliff, until the next wave paralyzed him for another instant.

Within minutes, Fred Benson was sprawled on his belly atop the cliff. He fastened a knot in the rope to a tree root, tied a rock into the other end, and lowered it down to the bow. Seamen Arthur Jansen of Superior and William Nyberg of Boston and wheelman John Borklund of Ashtabula had been up front with Benson and watched his startling leap and climb. One by one, they followed his rope to the cliff top. Benson helped by yanking the rope up the cliff. And one of the men brought a thicker rope up with him.

In the snow and wind, Benson hadn't said a word before his jump. And he didn't say much more now. All four shivering men assumed their crew mates in the stern had washed over with Morrow. They squinted into the dawn light, peering seventy-five feet down, toward the white cabin in the stern. They threw large rocks down to alert anyone who might still be alive, to wake them from a frozen slumber.

When he saw the cabin door swing open, Benson smiled through the ice and snow crusted around his face. They lowered the heavier rope, anchored with stones, and helped Captain Dissette and four others scale the cliff. Each one shivered and clung to Gold Rock as the waves battered on. But each made it to the top. They were freezing and hungry, chomping on snow to quench their burning thirst. The sky was growing lighter. Benson and the eight he'd rescued had no idea where they were.

As they headed into the woods, the 436-foot-long *Madeira*, now cleaved in two, sank into the choppy waters of Lake Superior.

VI

"The wind is the worst considering the length of time
it has been blowing and there is no promise of a let
up before evening."

~ Forecaster Herbert Richardson, November 28, 1905

Ever since the storm started to blow about seven o'clock that Monday night, Duluth was tossed into chaos. By eleven o'clock, the wind was clocked at sixty miles per hour from the northeast, screaming down from Hudson Bay and the Arctic beyond. It wasn't letting up. A green surge of Lake Superior rolled through the chutes of the Ship Canal piers, swamping the harbor and the Park Point area to the south.

As dangerous as it was out on the lake, Duluth's shoreline held its own perils. *Nasmyth* Captain Graham, heading to the ore dock at midnight, stumbled headfirst down a ravine. He lunged down a steep ten-foot bank to a debris pile of paving stones and ore. His nose split open from the forehead, and several bones in his face were shattered. He crawled to his boat, and later a horse-drawn ambulance took him to St. Mary's Hospital. If they could keep him alive, his face would be forever tattered.

Streetcar lines were iced over and service halted because the cars had no traction to get up the hills rimming the city. Telephone and telegraph poles snapped. Outhouses were carried away. Women and children stayed up past midnight, piling possessions in the street, fearing a giant wave would wash away their weathered lake-front homes.

The foghorn blew continuously. And that was no small feat. The new stone piers had been equipped with tunnels in case large seas washed over them. In this case, the tunnels flooded. That meant assistant lighthouse keeper James White was marooned all night, blasting the foghorn at the end of the south pier as waves crashed into the stone structure, sending spray one hundred feet in the air. He had no food or water but kept the foghorn whistling. The main keeper, James Prior, tried to relieve him but was twice washed off the south pier trying to dash to the pierhead light. People in town—and vessel men, for that matter—knew White was okay because the deep-throated yowl of the foghorn kept blowing.

The entrance to Duluth Harbor presents two wildly different faces during calm (pictured here in 1906) and during a storm (see Table of Contents). *Minnesota Historical Society*

The coal piles at the docks were awash from the brunt of the large waves, which covered the railroad tracks and standing train cars in up to three feet of lake water. The tug office, a wooden structure headquartering the Great Lakes Towing Company at slip No. 2, was flooded. At the corner of St. Croix Avenue and the railroad tracks, a pile of timbers and planks stood where a building once did. And next door, the back end of Ole Olson's saloon was wrecked from wave after wave battering the bar's wooden frame.

Ole's patrons, forced outside after midnight, saw the first boat attempting to return that Tuesday—the first of many. Crowds grew throughout Tuesday and bonfires were lit. More than ten thousand Duluthians eventually lined the beach and overlooks, elbowing each other for views from tall building windows.

When the *Arizona* appeared, riding the choppy waves about one o'clock in the morning, Ole's customers and other dockhands and sailors stood transfixed. Of all the ships to begin the harrowing series of chute-running that would captivate Duluth all day, the lumber-hauling *Arizona* was an improbable, quirky, and fitting vessel to go first.

Built in 1868 after the Civil War, the wooden hooker was only 189 feet long. It had seen steel-hulled ships, now three times its length, replace most of its old, artful wooden peers. In 1887, with a Duluth-bound cargo that included acid-filled iron tanks, the *Arizona* was enveloped by a storm off the Huron islands. The tanks broke free and spilled streams of acid, which caught flame. The riggings and deck were burning as the *Arizona* crept into Marquette, Michigan. Crewmembers—their clothes charred and their hair singed—jumped to the breakwater.

Nearly twenty years later, the *Arizona* found itself atop the crest of a giant wave at one o'clock in the morning, November 28, 1905. Captain Walter Neal couldn't see the lighthouse through the snow and fog and spray until he was two hundred feet away. But he'd headed as best he could toward the oonk-oonk of the fog whistle, waves splashing over the deck. The wind was simply too much. Like a spinning top, the *Arizona* whirled around three times. Just before the boat's timbers crunched, the improbable happened.

The bow was somehow pointing straight into the Ship Canal as a large wave pushed the *Arizona* into the harbor. Its rudder was smashed, but the engines started up again and drove the *Arizona* broadside through the canal to a tie-up at the Sixth Avenue dock. The captain racked it all up to pure luck.

It had been hours now since Herbert Richardson returned from his Master Mason ceremony at the Ionic Lodge. In his home office on the hill, the city forecaster heard the incessant wail of the foghorn and watched the graph paper record hour after hour of sixty-mile-per-hour wind. And he warned Duluthians, through the evening newspaper, not to be lulled or deceived if the skies quieted a bit that Tuesday afternoon. His maps, telegraphed from Washington until the lines went down, told him that the weather was shifting counterclockwise. Any break in the weather would be simply a hiatus foreshadowing the change to come. The northeast winds would soon

The 189-foot wooden hooker *Arizona* was the improbable first boat to successfully shoot the chutes of the Duluth piers in the early morning of November 28, 1905. *Historical Collections of the Great Lakes, Bowling Green State University*

be blowing blizzard-like across the prairies, blowing down the hills of Duluth and out into the lake. All the while, Richardson predicted the storm would bring blinding, powdery snow and the temperature would drop below zero.

"It may veer from the northeast to the northwest," Richardson told reporters shortly after midnight. "There is promise of heavy snowfall and the storm will, no doubt, go on record as one of the worst in recent years."

At 5:40 in the morning, Richardson's measuring equipment showed sustained winds, for ten minutes straight, blowing seventy miles per hour and whistling through the cracks in his window frames.

VII

"We were cold and hungry . . . so we applied for admittance at several houses, but were denied. We evidently scared people to death. I don't wonder any; I suppose we looked pretty tough."

~ *Crescent City* second mate H. J. Stephens
of London, Ontario

Arthur Daggett stood shivering alongside Buddemeyer and the other crewmembers of the *Crescent City*. The wet coats, sweaters, and britches hung heavily on their chilled bodies. Despite the predicament, Second Mate H. J. Stephens of London, Ontario, looked surprisingly stylish in high leather boots and a tam-o'-shanter with a wide, iced brim.

They all stood and stared at their huge boat with its white cabin, red hull, and silver smokestack that earned the *Crescent City* and the rest of the Pittsburgh Steamship fleet the nickname Tin Stackers. The snow was so heavy that they could only make out half of the steamer's four hundred feet. The silver smokestack on the stern was barely visible and seemed to have collapsed. All the upper rigging had been twisted. The whole ship groaned and creaked like a person in pain.

Water continued to pour into the midship crack, and the crew waited for the boat to be torn to pieces. But it settled in the cove. They knew how lucky they were. Had they struck the shore fifty yards in either direction, the *Crescent City* would have been a total wreck. They wouldn't be standing here in the snow, now shin-deep and banking higher.

Captain Rice and his first mate announced they would stay with the ship until daybreak. The rest of the crew was ordered to seek shelter and somehow get word to their bosses at the Pittsburgh Steamship Company office in the Wolvin Building in downtown Duluth. They had no idea where they were. But the glow in the distance, they guessed, was Duluth. Outlying homes couldn't be too far off. Stephens, in his high boots, led the way, followed by Buddemeyer. After more than a half hour walking with heads bent, shivering, they reached the Lakewood pumping station, where the graveyard shift engineer warmed them by his stove and offered them what dry clothes he could.

Andrew Johnson, the wheelman, took a group to the Lester Park neighborhood nearby, where he woke his mother. Stunned by the appearance of her visitors and groggy because of the early hour, she gladly offered shelter. Stephens and Buddemeyer left the pumping station on their own, hoping to find the telephone office. In the darkness and the blizzard, they lost their way.

So they pounded on predawn doors, both front doors and those in the back. Several times, they were turned away. Frightened homeowners peeked through curtains, saw the two men with faces black and iced, and figured they were highway robbers. Others were too sleepy to even come to the door.

"Who can blame them?" Stephens thought. He didn't bother talking to Buddemeyer, who might have heard him but probably couldn't. "As rough as we look," Stephens thought, "we're scaring people half to death."

Finally, they spotted a back kitchen shedding the faint light of a candle or stove. An older couple opened the back door of their simple wooden home. Buddemeyer explained they were sailors whose steamer had struck the rocks east of the Lakewood pumping station and the crew had been blessed by a miracle and all managed to make shore thanks to an old ladder and a lucky landing spot.

Stephens had forgotten how hungry he was. They hadn't eaten since Sault Sainte Marie the day before. So when the woman of the house offered coffee and bread, the boiling black liquid seemed to thaw his body from the inside. After all the people who had turned

The *Crescent City*'s port side hugs the beach. The ladder down which the crew scattered to shore appears to be faintly visible at midships. *Great Lakes Marine Collection of the Milwaukee Public Library/Wisconsin Marine Historical Society*

them away, Stephens felt his mood lighten along with the chill that had encased him for hours.

Stephens and Buddemeyer asked if they could use the telephone. The man shrugged. They didn't have a phone. But he offered them directions to the telephone office a mile away.

Warmed and upbeat, the two men headed out. The wind still swirled and the temperature surely had dropped below zero. Heads down, they trudged through the snow, finally finding the telephone office. Two women answered the door, with the chain lock in place.

Again, their heads shook and the door closed. The sailors had once again been turned away. Buddemeyer banged on the door until the younger of the women finally came back and said she wasn't to allow any strangers in until office hours and that was still four hours off.

With a nudge from Stephens' shoulder, the door opened and the chain lock fell in the snow. He apologized but said he was under strict orders to telephone Mr. H. W. Brown, the Pittsburgh Steamship Company agent, at the Wolvin Building downtown. The older woman gave in, dialed the four numbers, and handed Stephens the mouthpiece.

The line cracked in and out. They were only able to relay bits of information. Yes, all aboard the *Crescent City* had survived. But the boat was split and, mostly likely, about to break in two. They pleaded with the women to re-establish the connection. Finally, they gave up on the finicky gadget and plowed back through the snow toward downtown Duluth.

Stephens and Buddemeyer found a stable behind a home and woke the owner and begged him to hitch his team. No way, he said. He wasn't about to risk tangling his horses in the downed, crackling power lines for a couple of ruffians who said they were shipwreck survivors.

Despite all they'd been through in the last twenty-four hours, Stephens and Buddemeyer found it difficult to get angry with the man. They'd made it this far. One more shaking head wasn't going to dampen their spirit. But the wind was blowing full force, right off the lake, like it had been since seven o'clock the night before. Stephens and Buddemeyer, exhausted, spun around and lost their bearings.

They were soaked through again, chilled to the marrow, when they found Superior Drive and a working streetcar. The other passengers heading to work stared at them as if a spaceship had crashed in the storm with aliens from another planet. The car rattled for a half-mile before Stephens and Buddemeyer could make out the port of Duluth with its twin piers. They found the Wolvin Building, a brick structure along the harbor, and shared their story with Mr. Brown on the seventh floor.

Mr. Brown took the sailors across the street to the St. Louis Hotel and checked them in. He handed them a few dollars to buy some dry clothes. Just as Stephens and Buddemeyer walked down the wide steps of the hotel, a huge chunk of jagged sheet metal—pried off some nearby roof and lifted like a kite by the churning wind— narrowly missed their heads.

They laughed and laughed. Had they stepped out of the hotel a second earlier, they would have both been killed by the flying sheet of metal. After all they'd been through—the waves, the rocks, the ice, the snow, the slammed doors, the lost bearings—wouldn't that have been something? To get beheaded by an errant slice of roofing hurling through the morning streets of Duluth, just before buying warm clothes? Wouldn't that have been something?

VIII

"It will certainly be a happy day when we are rid of the whole bunch."

~ Pittsburgh Steamship Company President Harry Coulby, discussing the Marine Firemen, Oilers, and Water Tenders' Union in a 1904 letter

President Harry Coulby chartered a train when word of the storm's damage began dribbling into the new Cleveland headquarters of the Pittsburgh Steamship Company. Belching black smoke, the locomotive engine pulled a coach car, a business car, and two freight cars chock-full of pumps and wrecking equipment. Within thirteen hours, Coulby's special train would make it from Chicago to Duluth—eclipsing the old record by seventy-five minutes.

As the train headed north, Coulby could see the snow flickering in the darkness. He loved railroad tracks, the way they pointed so resolutely straight forward. He shared fine cigars with his marine superintendent, W. W. Smith, who would oversee salvage operations.

Coulby's square, paunchy face was only starting to show deep creases, running down from his pudgy nose to his thin, small lips. He was forty, although few men that age had crammed in so much.

President Harry Coulby ran
the Pittsburgh Steamship
Company with an iron fist.
Historical Collections of the
Great Lakes, Bowling Green
State University

Born on an English farm near Claypole on January 1, 1865, Coulby
spent his boyhood along the River Trent, which slices between
Lincolnshire and Nottinghamshire. He detested farm work and would
often lean on his hoe and listen to the train whistling in the distance.
He devoured library books with a passion but quit school at eleven.

At fourteen, he lit out, walking along the stone-fenced lanes to
Newark. For no pay, he learned the dits and dats of telegraphy at the
London, Midland & Scottish Railway. His pay climbed from twelve
to eighteen shillings when he moved to the big railroad office in Derby,
where trains rattled past, just as his chartered train car rattled through
the snowy darkness toward Minnesota twenty-two years later.

His mind drifted along with the cigar haze in his cabin. He didn't want to think about all his boats on the rocks in Lake Superior. At eighteen, Coulby had boarded his first ship, the steamer *Leonora*. Liverpool's harbor danced with tall sails and steam funnels on ships from across the globe. He stood at the rail, passing gaslit buoys until they were at sea for a month-long voyage to Cuba. He had landed a telegraph job there.

But Coulby was never comfortable in Santiago and contracted malaria within two weeks. His $800 annual salary from the West Indies and Panama Telegraph Company had sounded so good. But he shook with fever, his hand worthless on the telegraph equipment, and learned that his pay would start only after he'd earned enough to pay for the passage. He clashed with a senior clerk and finally sneaked on the steamship *Cienfuego* ("Fire Cloud"), stowing away to arrive in New York Harbor in March 1884.

Coulby's first stop in the land of opportunity was the charity wing of a Catholic hospital. When he recovered from malaria and convinced the nurses to discharge him, he started walking west. He'd read about America's Inland Seas. The name Great Lakes had fascinated him since he'd first gotten a whiff of them in the Claypole library.

Leaving New York on foot with his sea bag and the optimism April brings, Coulby followed railroad tracks to Albany and Buffalo. Working odd jobs for food, he picked his way six hundred miles to Cleveland.

The railroad tracks cutting through the blackness of late November 1905 must have reminded Coulby of those innocent days walking the rail beds, seeking his destiny.

When he arrived in Cleveland in 1884, the shipping season was going full tilt. He pushed through the sailors, ropes, horses, and carts to see the *Onoko*, the first big iron freighter on the Lakes. He climbed aboard the ship and asked for a deckhand's job. The first mate laughed. He had no room for an inexperienced, wide-eyed kid of nineteen.

There was plenty of work downtown, though, pushing wheelbarrows and helping a construction crew put an addition on the old courthouse. Cleveland, like so many American cities, was beginning to flourish, perched at it was between the steel foundries of Pittsburgh and the thousand-mile highway of Great Lakes water between Duluth and Buffalo.

Coulby hated pushing his wheelbarrow up ramps all day. It reminded him of the farm work back home. So he attended a commercial school to learn how to operate a new device called the typewriter and practiced shorthand on Sundays. By fall 1884, he'd landed a stenographer job for the Lake Shore & Michigan Railway.

Two decades later, he would be zooming through the frigid Midwest darkness as president of the lake arm of U.S. Steel. But when he turned twenty, Harry Coulby was writing a different kind of history.

Amasa Stone had built the railway for which Coulby worked. Stone had two daughters. One married John Hay, President Abraham Lincoln's aging former secretary. Hay needed help amassing a dozen-volume biography of Lincoln and hired Coulby to sort through stacks of unkempt manuscripts.

Coulby took dictation from the old man. He loved the stories of Lincoln using homespun tales to drive points home. He checked facts, perused documents, and transcribed Hay's notes. The old man tried to bring Coulby along to Washington when their project was complete, but Coulby was uninterested.

Amasa Stone's other daughter had married Samuel Mather, one of the early finance giants behind the merged industry powerhouse that was forging into U.S. Steel. Hay called Mather and, for $50 a month, Coulby hired on with the Pickands Mather and Company in Cleveland's Western Reserve Building. He was soon immersed in the competitive world of rival fleets, floating freight rates, volatile weather, and feisty unions.

Things were changing in American business, and Coulby was ready to cash in. U.S. Steel came together in 1901, a complicated merger involving barons with names such as Rockfeller, Carnegie, and J. P. Morgan. This first American megacorporation soon consolidated most of the Great Lakes shipping interests, which for years had been a fiercely independent fleet of sailing vessels.

Coulby first took over a string of whalebacks, funny-looking ships that sailors called pig boats. They floated low in the water, like some plump cousin of the submarine. But they required as many men as the much larger steamers, which soon eclipsed the inefficient pig boats. The first two steamers Coulby had built he named in honor of Amasa Stone and Samuel Mather.

Coulby always tried to remember from where he came. But things were happening at a dizzying pace. By 1904, Coulby was running the Pittsburgh Steamship Company, U.S. Steel's massive 112-ship armada. If linked stem to stern, the ships would cover eight miles of waterway. He also controlled what would become the Interlake Fleet, not to mention the Great Lakes Towing Company.

Coulby liked to walk along the gaslit waterfront, where massive loads of iron ore were shuttled nonstop from the docks of Duluth and Two Harbors down to the blast furnaces of Ohio. He'd often join the crews of his boats to learn firsthand about navigating channels, changing weather, and the ship workers' unions that increasingly irritated him. He'd been a worker himself, so Coulby could relate to the men. But he grew increasingly ruthless as his empire mushroomed.

At the same time, Coulby loved to chew cigars and spin stories about Mrs. Plumtree and his goat-tending neighbor, Bingham, back home on his farm in England. He'd always insist on expensive English-tailored suits, but he'd flip some gold and silver coins to any nun who would ask for charity. He often made his weeks in the paupers' hospital in New York the subject of his moral-charged yarns.

Business subordinates called him the Old Man before he turned forty. Like Lincoln, Coulby battered associates with bromides. At teatime, he told colleagues to spread the butter thin because it tasted as good and lasted longer, a lesson learned from his mother. Around the table, he was a bulldog, demanding to know what you got—and you and you.

"The horse didn't leave much in the stable this morning," he'd chastise lazy aides.

Coulby controlled more than 110 vessels on the lakes, a fleet larger than the U.S. Navy. He was pivotal in rate pricing and had two ideas to fatten his company's huge profits. He took on the unions to win the battle over who really controlled the ships that were increasing in number, size, and scope on the Great Lakes in the early 1900s.

And Coulby boosted efficiency by phasing out the smaller boats and the barges they towed. The longer the ships, the more money could be made with the same size crews. As the old wooden schooners all but vanished from the Great Lakes, so did the need for skilled sailors. The new, steel steamships coming out of yards were floating factories at four hundred, then five hundred, then six hundred feet long.

The massive ships needed firemen shoveling wheelbarrow after wheelbarrow of coal at hellacious speed. And oilers and watchmen, mates and ship masters. But gone were the days of a schooner captain hiring his crew, knowing each man's special sailing talents—be they knot tying or compass reading.

Harry Coulby made one thing clear in this new corporate era. Management called the shots. The honchos in Cleveland hired captains and assigned them to the steamers. They made every important call in a uniform culture that clashed with the independent days of lake hauling. Cleveland, Coulby's new handpicked base of operation for Pittsburgh Steamship Company, would be the epicenter of lake power for decades.

Duluth, the Lakes' westernmost outpost, quickly felt Coulby's presence. Built on the steep Lake Superior hillside, Duluth's population climbed 20 percent between 1900 and 1905 as the rich ore deposits of the Iron Range brought money to the north country. The Old Man down in Cleveland fired some men in the company's Duluth office as part of U.S. Steel's financial streamlining. He slashed auditing clerks' pay from $125 a month to $60 and reduced other salaries by a quarter.

Unions had a spotty record on the Great Lakes in the late 1800s. With more new boats splashing out of the yards, jobs were plentiful. But the chasm between ranks grew larger.

Ship captains, mates, and engineers were licensed and well paid, but firemen, deckhands, oilers, cooks, and stewards were paid poorly, treated harshly, and offered no hope for improvement. The good jobs were fore; the lousy work aft.

If they didn't like the jobs, plenty of men on the docks were willing to take them. These lower-ranked grunts were hired one trip at a time and kicked loose if the ship stayed in port. Not surprisingly, the unsteady conditions attracted a vagabond, carousing, lowlife breed of characters.

Firemen—who shoveled coal into furnaces for low pay—tended to be the rogues of the bunch. They would jump ship without notice, report to duty drunk, and destroy their bodies by keeping hard-firing boats going at full speed.

The Marine Firemen's Union was among the first Coulby locked in his sights. He took over the fleets' Lake Carriers' Association, which cut wages and gave vessels authority to lay off oilers, deckhands, and firemen if they were in port for three days. Coulby eliminated engineer jobs on the barges towed behind the big freighters. He pressured the Seaman's Union to drop overtime rules and broke the Marine Cooks and Stewards Union with a flat-rate offer of $70 per month for chief cooks.

Coulby's major fight wasn't in the lower ranks, though, where cooks and firemen were typically happy just to be working. Wresting control of the boats themselves was Coulby's main drive. And that meant busting the captains' union, the American Association of Masters and Pilots.

In 1904, Coulby required captains to reapply for their jobs. The masters fought back, demanding the right to organize and asking for annual salaries of $2,250 for piloting the largest ships. They wanted to be paid for nine months, never mind if weather cut the season short, and the only transfers they'd go along with would be to larger boats.

Coulby urged his fellow fleet bosses to say "No." Captains were merely the owners' representatives onboard. The companies would control these massive freighters. The days of the independent schooners were history.

Masters responded by initiating a strike in the early shipping season of 1904, but Coulby and others convinced some of the younger captains to continue working. That spooked older captains, fearing they'd lose their ships. By June 14, the strike was over. Coulby had won. By the next year, he was paying captains between $1,540 and $1,980 depending on the size of the boat they mastered. He did allow them to pick their own mates—subject to approval at headquarters in Cleveland and on the condition that there would be no "unionists" in the lot.

Coulby had managed this storm, muting the roar of labor unions and organizing all the tentacles of Great Lakes shipping under one umbrella. Now he had another storm to deal with. A real storm of snow and wind and subzero temperatures. The number of Tin

Stackers damaged on this last run of 1905 kept climbing with every update at every station where his fast train stopped. The *Crescent City* was the first to hit the rocks. But dozens more ships were out in this storm.

IX

"The elements are quite a lot bigger than anything the hands of man can build."

~ Captain Richard W. England, December 9, 1905

As Coulby's train zoomed toward Duluth at record speed, Fred J. Cosford stood outside his home on Minnesota Avenue near 26th Street. That's out on Minnesota Point, a thin ribbon of beachy land that separates Lake Superior from the harbor in the miles south of the pier opening. It was pushing noon that Tuesday, and Cosford had never seen anything like the steamer that towered in front of him:

"She was high in the air on the crest of an enormous wave which seemed to descend more rapidly than she for I could see daylight under her for seconds as it seemed."

He ducked behind the fence in front of his house and cringed, fearing the freighter would strike the beach. Then Fred Cosford took off running. His boots stuck in the slushy sand of the beach. He pulled them out of the frozen quicksand and pushed on. He had to alert Captain Murdoch McLennan, head of the Duluth station of the U.S. Life-Saving Service.

McLennan was built like a moose, born in Scotland, forty-three years old. He'd been a lifesaver for eighteen years, working for the outfit that was a precursor to the U.S. Coast Guard. And the job wasn't getting any easier. Procuring surfboats, line-shooting cannons, and other equipment always involved a frustrating tangle of red tape. And most of the other experienced lifesavers in the service were bolting for better paying jobs on the docks and boats that were roaring with business and money. Replacements McLennan made to his crew often seemed to be less and less experienced and have sketchier character. He'd had to fire several for various sins committed inside and outside the saloons of Duluth.

When Fred Cosford, breathless and panting, arrived at McLennan's little station a mile up the beach, he wasn't even sure which boat had been tossed on the shore. McLennan didn't care either. He called his ragamuffin crew to order. And they headed south toward the Oatka Beach Pavilion, dragging their equipment, including ropes and a little cannon to shoot breeches buoys for a rescue procedure they practiced endlessly on the beach. This was no drill. The crew had to pull apparatus over fallen trees, around downed trolley wires and telegraph poles.

Captain Murdoch McLennan directed Duluth's U.S. Life-Saving Service, a precursor to the Coast Guard, from 1898 until 1915. *U.S Coast Guard Historian's Office*

The 363-foot *R. W. England*, built the year before, had left the Soo Locks at eight o'clock Sunday night, light for a last load of ore. The *England* was piloted by a man with the same name, six-year-captain Richard England. He'd been promoted in 1899 when he was the first mate on the *V. H. Ketchum*. The wealthy owner of the ship liked to travel incognito, and Captain England impressed him with his leadership and courage.

England—his thin black hair parted down the middle of a receding hairline, his mustache bushy—had seen plenty of big storms. During his first year as a master, he was out on Lake Erie during what become known as the Galveston Typhoon. Earlier in his career, after a long ocean crossing, England was stuck in the Irish Sea for forty hours, waiting for the wind to let up. The Galveston storm had reminded him of that gale, only worse.

When the wind started to blow that Monday night, the *England* was rounding Keweenaw Point, the thumb of land jutting out of Lake Superior's southern coast. The blinding snow made it impossible to see anything. Waves were climbing the after house at the back of the boat and filling the empty hold, giving some needed ballast. The waves flooded the crew quarters, sending the twenty-one aboard scurrying. At four o'clock in the morning, England ordered the men to don their cork-stuffed life preservers.

Captain England caught a glimpse of the shore about eight o'clock that morning and fought the wind and wave toward Duluth. About eleven that morning, a huge wave swept away the ship's manhole covers and crashed in cabin doors and windows. England had never been caught in such wild seas.

He tried everything. He ordered his wheelman to crank to the port side and telegraphed to the engine room for full speed, repeating the message several times. When he saw the trees on the shore, England ordered the anchors dropped and tried to back up at full speed. All the maneuvering didn't matter. The *England* had missed the three-hundred-foot gap between the piers of the Duluth Ship Canal, which jutted two thousand feet out from the harbor.

When the captain tried to nose the ship back out into the lake for another shot at the chutes, a giant wave smacked the *England*'s starboard side and tossed her onto the beach. Spectators along the point gasped—including Fred Cosford.

By 2:30 that Tuesday afternoon, McLennan and his lifesaving crew had responded to the wail of the *England*'s distress whistles and to Cosford's eyewitness account of the beaching. Lifesavers fired their breeches buoy aboard the ship, and five deckhands and three oilers took up Captain England's offer that anyone who wanted to go ashore was welcome. The boat was beached firmly, with little danger, so most of the men stayed aboard rather than risk the daring ride down the rope chair. The lifesaving crew worked efficiently, and only one of the nine men who climbed into the carriage wound up getting dunked when the ship suddenly listed and dipped him into the water. Captain England went to shore and reported the events to his transit company and spoke with reporters, including the young woman, Mary McFadden. When she asked if he expected to ever see another such gale on the Great Lakes, England shrugged and fiddled with his thick mustache:

"I hope it is the last of its kind as it was the first."

He lamented missing the ship canal, but then again: "It may be for the best after all. It is better to be where we are than to have met distress at the canal."

X

"There was a rash of spectators to the canal . . . every available vantage point was black with people who waited almost breathlessly. . . ."

"And a curious crowd it was, this motley gathering. . . . There were capitalists and horny-handed sons of toil, school girls and wantons, sailors and land lubbers."

~ Duluth Evening Herald, November 28 and 29, 1905

As Tuesday's tempest played out on Lake Superior, crowds amassed along the Duluth harbor, their curiosity blending the instincts of both the Good Samaritan and the vulture. More than one hundred people elbowed for views in the sun parlor of the Spaulding Hotel, the heartier ones spilling onto the windswept rooftop. Those with marine glasses called out what they saw, while men and women, dressed in fine Victorian clothing, squinted through the falling snow toward the maelstrom of lake waves and heaving currents.

Dozens of onlookers streamed down to the canal for a closer look. Groups on the beach lit towering bonfires that would burn all night long, as both a navigational aid to captains on the lake and a heat source for the gawkers.

A 1905 view of Duluth's Superior Street shows the Spaulding Hotel on the right. *Courtesy of the* Minneapolis Star Tribune *library*

Shortly after one o'clock that Tuesday afternoon, about an hour after the *England* had been shoved onto the sandy bottom, the neck-craning crowd two miles north caught a glimpse of the smokestack and masts of the *Isaac L. Ellwood* tossing in the towering water. Another Tin Stacker of Harry Coulby's Pittsburgh Steamship fleet, the 478-foot steamer was loaded with ore. The day before, at about four o'clock Monday afternoon, the *Ellwood* had sailed past the gaslights on the piers and out of Duluth when the wind was fresh and Lake Superior was tranquil. The boat was heading up the North

Shore to Two Harbors to pick up a barge and sail in tandem to Lake Erie. When the gale struck, the snow quickly became too thick to see the Two Harbors lighthouse.

Captain C. H. Cummings figured he'd ride out the blow off Two Harbors, but wave after wave flooded the *Ellwood*'s deck, ripping off tarpaulins meant to cover the hatches. Crewmembers scurried to tie down the tarps. Cummings cringed as some were nearly swept off the boat. At eight o'clock Monday night, he decided to try to turn the big boat around and run back toward Duluth. Turning a steamer nearly five hundred feet long through peaks and valleys of a darkened Lake Superior is no simple maneuver. Even a boat filled with ore could capsize in weather that awful, like a child's bathtub toy.

The *Arizona*, the little wooden hooker that spun through the canal at midnight, reported seeing the *Ellwood* near the Apostle Islands sometime during the long previous night. Making headway through the choppy waves was tedious. But about one o'clock that afternoon, the *Ellwood* appeared in the snowy offing. The hordes of people lining the Duluth Ship Canal and straining to see from hotel rooftops and parlors cheered and gasped—depending on their dispositions.

The *Ellwood* plowed toward the canal at slow speed. The onlookers grew quiet as waves swamped the bow one minute and submerged the stern the next, unleashing blasts of white spray. Captain Cummings feared the tumbling currents at the mouth of the canal, where water surging in and out of the chutes rammed into the wind-raked waves. Cummings ordered his engineer, who in turn messaged his firemen, to open up and use all 250 pounds of steam pressure.

It didn't work. The current and a huge wave banged the *Ellwood*'s bow into the concrete and stone of the north pier head. Spectators' jaws gaped. The collision snapped some of the boat's steel plates. But in the end, it was more of a glancing blow than a direct punch. The *Ellwood* nosed the pier again, hitting just in front of its boiler room, busting more plates.

The double hit sent the boat nearly broadside across the 300-foot canal opening. With full steam running, the *Ellwood* swung itself around and moved safely into the harbor. Deckhands tossed heavy rope lines to waiting tugboats.

The people on the piers and rooftops let loose a hearty cheer. Men waved their hats and jumped into each other's arms. Echoing their delight, the harbor tugs belched out a string of celebratory whistles. *Ellwood* crewmembers clasped their hands together over their heads like the victorious prizefighters of the era. Even Captain Cummings waved from the bridge as the *Ellwood* answered all the euphoria with the loud, clear groan of its own whistle.

The tugs pulled the boat to the shallows near the Duluth Boat Club. Water poured into the sluices ripped open by the pier, and the

Ellwood settled in twenty-two feet of water, its pilot house just above the waves. The crew was plucked off and ferried to the docks. After all the giddy celebrating, the onlookers on the rooftops and piers strained to see through the snow again. About two o'clock that afternoon, November 28, 1905, the *Mataafa* appeared, steaming toward the three-hundred-foot gap between the stone piers.

PART 3

The Mataafa

I

God give us all for the glad New Year
Spirit to pity, spirit to cheer
Soul for service and kindly heart
Disposition to lift our part
Of the common burden, and do our share
Of the common work, and our trials bear
With silence and courage, and show us how
To turn to trouble a dauntless brow,
Reveal to us all the kindly grace,
And good in the average neighbor's face—
God give us all, in the glad New Year,
Spirit to love, and spirit to cheer!

~ Mary D. McFadden, *Duluth News Tribune*,
January 1, 1905

"The waves were tossing the Mataafa as if she were a birch canoe."

~ Ernest Dietz, deckhand, Winnipeg, Manitoba
November 29, 1905

Mataafa Captain Dick Humble smiles with a cigar in calmer times in 1904. *J. W. Westcott Co. Archives*

They were mostly in their twenties, the two dozen crewmembers aboard the *Mataafa*. Even Captain Dick Humble, at thirty-two, had a boyish smile of porcelain teeth and a mop of curly brown hair. His wife, Jessie, and baby daughter, Bernice, were waiting for him in their home at 229 Hill Street in Conneaut, Ohio—a Lake Erie town near Cleveland, across Lake Superior, through the Soo Locks, down Lake Huron, past Detroit, on the south shore. Not far away, the blast furnaces were waiting for the load of iron ore in the belly of Humble's steamship.

The *Mataafa* looked powerful but had undersized engines. *Historical Collections of the Great Lakes, Bowling Green State University*

In the back on the 430-foot-long *Mataafa*, assistant engineer James Early had just received word that his bride had borne him a daughter back in Buffalo. He was sailing home to see her. Chief engineer William Most called Cleveland home but kept in his pocket receipts of registered letters to his wife in Chicago, where she waited out the long season with relatives. And cook Walter Bush from Amherstburg, Ontario, one of three black men aboard, spoke of his wife and kids.

But most of the men were single, roving spirits, who came from all over the map for the wages to be squeezed out of a final Thanksgiving week run across the Inland Seas. Tom McCloud, a deckhand from Kentucky, had signed on just a week before in Conneaut. Captain Humble had stopped there to visit his family and added fireman Thomas Woodgate, as well. His muscles were sculpted like thick rope from months of shoveling coal, making him one of the finest human specimens Humble had hired in his six years at the helm. Woodgate carried a letter in his pocket from his father, fretting over stormy weather.

Like its crew, the boat was young, built in Ohio six years earlier just as Humble was promoted to master. At first, the steamer was called the *Pennsylvania*, but after a few runs in 1899, it was rechristened the *Mataafa*—the name of a recent Samoan king. The new name painted high on its red bow plates and across its stern corresponded with the Minnesota Steamship Company's system of starting boats with the prefix "Ma" and ending with the letter "a." The *Madeira*, twenty-five miles north and zeroing in on Gold Rock, carried the same coding.

At 430 feet long and 50 feet wide, the *Mataafa* was a big but simple boat. A white pilot house stood in front, often called the forecastle because it looked like a castle with a dental tooth–like top rail. Although considered a modern ship when it was built, by 1905 it

The heavy hatch covers punctuating the *Mataafa*'s deck divided its forecastle and stern into two different worlds. *Great Lakes Marine Collection of the Milwaukee Public Library/Wisconsin Marine Historical Society*

A *Mataafa* sailor sits on a hatch cover in 1904 with the bow behind him. *J. W. Westcott Co. Archives*

The *Mataafa* waits in the Soo Locks in 1904. The black crewmembers looking over the rail in the forefront may be cook Walter Bush and steward Henry Wright. *J. W. Westcott Co. Archives*

Mataafa crewmembers hose down the deck in 1904. *J. W. Westcott Co. Archives*

lacked some of the design elements popular in the newer boats splashing out of the shipyards.

For one thing, the stern had no deck house. The *Mataafa* instead had what was known as a submarine stern, in which the galley and crew quarters were tucked below deck in the hull of the boat. Twelve hatches punctuated the long deck. Unlike newer steamers, the *Mataafa* still used heavy hardwood hatch covers that rested on coamings and stayed in place by their weight alone. At eight feet long and three feet wide, these wooden covers were loathed by sailors and stevedores, who had to lug the bulky beasts on and off and store them while the boat was being loaded. The engine was modest: 1,200 horsepower. Many of the more powerful engines in the Pittsburgh fleet had been pulled out to go into the new, larger boats at the shipyards.

And while newer vessels featured hidden tunnels for crewmembers to move from stem to stern in bad weather, the *Mataafa* had only its sweeping deck and exposed gangway in the after section in back. A two-wire rail fence, about waist high, ran the length of the deck's edge. Two masts with riggings stood toward each end, reminders of the wooden ships and fluttering sails all but eclipsed by these steel, steam-powered bulk freighters.

The higher-paid members of the crew—Humble, his mates, wheelmen, and watches—stayed up front. The captain's quarters included stained wood and a bathtub. The firemen, oilers, cook, porter, and steward stayed in the back of the boat, where the top of the silver smokestack was painted black to mask the soot. This was the trademark of the Pittsburgh Steamship Company, the new mega-corporation now four years old. U.S. Steel's lake-shipping subsidiary, with Harry Coulby calling the shots, had gobbled up the Minnesota Steamship Company and other lines of independent freighters. With more than one hundred Tin Stackers in the fleet, the boats formed an almost constant chain of smoke-spewing steamers hauling ore, produce, and lumber across the Great Lakes.

Humble enjoyed a good cigar. He chewed on one that Monday afternoon, weighing all the factors. Herbert Richardson's storm flags were hoisted at the pier, but Humble had lived on the Inland Seas for sixteen years, including six as a master. He couldn't help but trust his gut over the science of meteorology. He'd heeded the warnings for four days, waiting out the last blow. But his crew was itching to sail, as were his bosses at the Pittsburgh Steamship. They'd suffered through a disappointing season, hurt by a rash of storms. Humble knew it was his call when to go. The bosses urged him to use good sense when gauging weather conditions and not put his steamer at undue risk or peril.

Yet an unseen pressure existed, a drive for profits and a grow-ing sense of economic ruthlessness. Corporate powerhouses, such as Harry Coulby, were busting unions and imposing regulations. All of it left cigar-chomping captains like Dick Humble feeling less and less in control of their vessels.

Humble tried to remember a big whopper of a storm that hadn't been followed by some days of calm. He couldn't. To him, it always seemed as if nature, having exhaled so prodigiously, needed time to inhale. Humble smiled. It was time to go. He flicked cigar ash into the dirty water of Duluth harbor. The *Mataafa* would sail at 3:30 that Monday afternoon, with the 366-foot barge *James Nasmyth* towed in consort.

Black smoke trailed from the smokestack as the *Mataafa* began its journey, slicing between the long stone piers dotted with gaslit lamps. The piers functioned as wide sidewalks with chest-high walls on each side, where passersby in hoop skirts and smart hats often ambled out to watch the boats come and go. The wind was fresh, blowing in from the northeast. The waves lapped as gently as those in a mid-sized pond. Captain Humble offered the customary farewell toot of three long whistles followed by two shorts ones.

Despite the calm, Humble had an anxious feeling. The barometer had been too high on Sunday. He didn't like to see a reading so high; once it started to fall, there was no telling how far it could plummet.

His first mate, Wally Brown, looked at the glass. "Still falling, Captain."

After a stint of smooth sailing, Humble stood behind the window of the white pilot house, figuring they had reached a point abreast of Two Harbors. He watched as the snow started to fall at 7:30 that Monday night. The waves began to rise into choppy combers as the wind gained speed, spraying the deck and forecastle windows.

The *Mataafa* plodded through the thickening snow, at about seven miles per hour, until two o'clock in the morning. By then, the gale had blown into something neither Humble nor his crew had ever encountered—or would ever forget.

He noted the time in the forepeak—two o'clock in the morning—and made a mental note: "The sea had gotten so large that it was running over our decks from both sides, loosening the hatch fastenings."

Humble ordered his wheelman, George McClure, to crank the boat hard aport and snug toward shore, but the wind blew the vessel around and the blizzard blinded them. If anyone stepped out on the deck, he might see the finger at the end of his arm, but no farther. Humble rang the engine room and asked Bill Most, his engineer, to work the engines as strong as possible. After an hour, the big boat was back "head to the wind."

The waves were as high as Humble had ever seen. While he stood in the forecastle and watched waves tumble over the deck from both sides, the crew aft shoveled coal, manned the engine-room levers, and hunkered into their quarters. The acrid smell of smoke and the relentless noise of wind and waves battered their senses.

When the pitching jostled a cupboard door latch in the galley, dozens of plates flew out and shattered. Then lake water began crashing through porthole windows, flooding crew quarters and gangways with frozen slush.

Down below, firemen Thomas Woodgate, Charlie Byrne, Axel Carlson, and Ed Coulter struggled to stay on their feet, shoveling coal as fast as they could into the flaming boilers. In conditions like these, the boats became two distinct worlds. The pilot house up front and the engine room aft were separated by a vast and dangerous middle world: the wave-swept, icy deck. The wire rails looked overmatched in their battle to keep anyone from washing overboard. One other device connected the white forecastle to the submarine stern. A Chadburn communication system allowed the pilot house to signal instructions to the engineers aft. Humble kept ordering full steam until four o'clock in the morning.

At times, the *Mataafa* found itself on the bottom of sea troughs, with walls of water on both sides sweeping the deck. At five o'clock in the morning, Humble again called Bill Most on the Chadburn and asked for all the power he had. With the wheel now hard starboard, Humble realized it was impossible to get ahead anymore.

They tossed around, about twenty miles east of Two Harbors, when Humble made the first in a series of decisions that would be critiqued and analyzed for decades to come.

Just off Sandy Island, he whistled the *Nasmyth* and word spread among the crew. He was giving up the fight. A dozen hours after leaving Duluth, they would swing around in the wind and retreat, circling back from where they had come: the chutes of the Duluth Ship Canal.

The men cheered Humble's call. They wanted to see baby daughters in Buffalo, wives in Chicago. They wanted to sink their teeth into the white, juicy breasts of Thanksgiving turkey. They were hungry and thirsty. It had been too hard for the men up front to venture to the water tanks in the stern. Mostly, they just wanted off the lake. So when Humble gave the word and let the steamer swing around before the wind, an upbeat mood swept across the deck along with the icy waves.

Humble issued strict orders that no one was to wander out on the deck or away from the cabins. Such a step would have been suicidal as waves continuously lapped between the hatches.

About eight o'clock Tuesday morning, the sky a pale pewter and shrouded in thick fog and snow, the men could hear the Two Harbors whistle. Again, their spirits were buoyed. But the visibility remained poor. Humble considered his options again. He could make a run for the shelter of Two Harbors, but he couldn't see a thing. He feared disaster, steaming blind into a cramped port. So he hollered at his wheelman, the brawny, athletic George McClure: "Crank the wheel hard astarboard. Let's try to get windward again."

That didn't work. The storm simply had more power than the *Mataafa*'s engines. So after a fruitless hour trapped in the trough of the sea, unable to get head to the wind, Humble ordered the wheel put hard aport. They came around the other way, heading toward the rocky North Shore between Two Harbors and Duluth.

Humble let the wind push the boat and waited for the seas to go down and the snow to clear up. The fastenings were giving way, and he feared he would lose the dozen large wooden hatch covers. He had to find shelter soon. But as bad as things were in the blizzard's frenzy, Humble and the crew also knew a collision with land would be worse than being tossed around out on the lake.

He put out the word to lower 30 fathoms, or 180 feet, of anchor chain. They would stand off until the weather eased. The lake was dangerous but safer than risking a shore landing. And the weather was bound to break soon. It had been blowing fiercely for sixteen hours now. Humble's instincts told him it would die down.

Bush, the cook, put some food in the galley, where a noontime dinner was typically a high point of the day. But the men were too cold and scared to have an appetite. They snatched a few bites on the run.

At noon, the snow eased and Humble and his mate, Wally Brown, could see Duluth rising from the faint outline of the shore. It seemed quite close. As they gazed through the marine glass, the Duluth skyline came into focus below the city's rimmed hillsides.

When Humble looked back over his shoulder, though, he could see that the hatch bars were buckling. The heavy wooden lids meant to protect the iron ore cargo from nasty elements were giving way. He ordered McClure to turn hard aport. They would make a run for Duluth and the long piers that jutted out like a sleepwalker's arms.

The crowds had swelled on the piers, the beaches, the rooftops, and inside the office buildings and hotels on Superior Street. The *E. C. Pope* appeared off the piers at two o'clock that Tuesday afternoon. A dozen or so onlookers watched from the U.S. Hydrographic Office on the top of the Torrey Building. At times, they gasped as the *Pope* seemed to swamp, vanishing from view. Then the smokestack would pop up again.

Even though its steering had been damaged in the gale, forcing the *Pope*'s crew at the back to guide the ship by hand, it foamed through the center of the canal chutes. Buffeting waves prevented the steamer from striking one pier, then the other. A puffing tug greeted the *Pope*, as did the celebratory salutes of the whistling steamers in the harbor and the cheers of the spectators.

Captain Humble had seen the *Pope* out in the tempest of Lake Superior the night before. He was now two miles behind, heading for the harbor and the ship canal's narrow, three-hundred-foot chasm. The little wooden *Arizona* had shot the chutes, as the sailors liked to say. And the *Ellwood* and the *Pope* had somehow managed the gauntlet as well. Only the *England* had missed, beaching harmlessly two miles south, luring Captain Murdoch McLennan and his life-savers down the sandy spit of Park Point to fetch the crew.

Humble knew nothing of the *Arizona*, *Ellwood*, *Pope*, or *England*. He was now fixated on his barge, the *Nasymth*, heaving up and down behind him with its own cargo of ore. The barge's fate had been literally tied to the *Mataafa*'s. Until now.

The decisions to leave Duluth that Monday, to turn around twelve hours later, to skip past Two Harbors, to run for Duluth—all those dilemmas had been a snap compared to the matter now weighing on Humble's mind. He was convinced he had to drop the towline connecting the *Mataafa* and the *Nasmyth*. Together, they had survived the worst gale any man on either boat had ever witnessed. But there was simply no sea room to navigate even his own 430-foot steel steamer through the stone piers in these heaving conditions. Trying to shoot the chutes with a barge in tow risked a collision that could destroy both vessels.

But before he blew for the barge to prepare its anchors and shorten its towline, Humble paused. He felt like an executioner before squeezing a firing line trigger. He knew this was his only recourse. He also knew the storm was too powerful for the *Nasmyth* to ride out at anchor. The barge would dash upon the rocks of the beach, unless some tug could get to it first. But that seemed impossible with all the surges and waves and currents crisscrossing the canal opening.

With a heavy heart, Humble made up his mind on two fronts. He sent his second mate, Herbert Emigh, aft with orders to drop the towline and let the barge go. He then blew for the *Nasmyth* to drop its anchors.

Humble rang up the Chadburn, requesting more steam from the engine room, which meant more coal from the firemen. The *Mataafa* burrowed down the shore, aiming straight at the narrow canal opening. Behind it, the *Nasmyth* drifted alone, its anchors dragging along the lake bottom like the claws of a faithful dog trying to resist being pulled away from its master.

II

"The harbor seemed to offer the only chance to escape destruction and the captain determined to make a run for the inside at all hazards."

~ The United States Life-Saving Service annual report,
fiscal year ending June 30, 1906

The barge no longer tethered, the *Mataafa* churned at full speed toward the center of the canal. Humble feared the currents that swirled unpredictably at the mouth of the chutes. Often crossways to the wind, the surging current was now gushing northward. Humble gave orders to head as nearly as possible to the middle of the canal.

The boat's steering was working fine. Everything was going well. An optimistic spirit welled up as Humble gazed out the pilot house window, Duluth growing closer. He tried to suppress a smile as the long boat inched into the three-hundred-foot opening between two-thousand-foot parallel piers stretching out to greet him. But he knew his hellish journey wasn't over yet.

As the strong current nudged the *Mataafa* toward the north pier, a monstrous wave lifted the stern. Onlookers gulped. Like a spearfisher, the wave thrust the nose of the boat under the surface. The bow struck the muddy, rock-strewn lake bottom.

With a shudder from stem to stern, the *Mataafa* sheered starboard. Humble hollered for wheelman George McClure to turn the steamer harder astarboard, hoping to veer right and clear the north pier. But the boat had already drifted too close. The nose of the *Mataafa* crept inside the end of the north pier. And it struck with a booming jolt, a hard blow on the bluff of the starboard bow.

Monstrous waves crashed in pilot house windows, the splintered glass cutting McClure's wrists and hands at the wheel. McClure held on despite oozing blood and water swirling up to his waist at times. He tried to crank the wheel hard to the port side to get the *Mataafa* off the pier and out into the open channel. But the waves were too strong and the boat not powerful enough.

Fireman Charlie Byrne from Detroit was working in the engine room. He heard a sickening thud and listened as the engine made a strange whirring noise. He knew what that meant—as did all of the dozen men in the rear end of the *Mataafa*. The steering was shot. The wheel was gone.

Up front, Humble rang his Chadburn to order more power. But Bill Most, the chief engineer who mailed letters to his wife in Chicago, sent back ominous word from the engine room. They'd lost power. He couldn't get the engine to work. The wheel was gone, perhaps because something had shoved up between its blades. Water flooded the lower gangway in the stern, dousing the fire in the boilers.

"It's all up, boys," Most shouted as the men dashed up to the aft deck. They found themselves slipping in a foot of icy slush. Bone-chilling spray pelted and drenched them as they tried to find protection behind the silver smokestack and among the bent ventilator tubes.

The *Mataafa*, now powerless, sprawled broadside across the piers, facing south.

Continuing to swing around with no way to control its course, the long boat met the north pier, forming a T-bone that battered the steel hull with each wave.

The Mataafa strikes the Duluth pier on November 28, 1905. The steamship broke in half while 10,000 Duluthians watched helplessly from shore. *Photo by Hugh McKenzie, Lake Superior Maritime Collections, UW–Superior*

Waves sweep over the *Mataafa* at the height of the storm, separating the men fore and aft. *Photo by Hugh McKenzie, Lake Superior Maritime Collections, UW–Superior*

Humble could easily make out the shore through the swirling snowflakes. He saw the throngs of people and the bonfires they'd built. His mind quickly turned to the lifeboats tethered to the sides of the *Mataafa*. They could certainly ferry his hungry, shivering men to shore. The distance seemed so short. The St. Louis Hotel, with its warm brandy, thick blankets, and crackling fireplaces, was so near.

The yawl boat, dangling off the port side toward the open lake, could take a dozen men. But as each wave banged the starboard side into the pier, the waves smashed the yawl boat to pieces. A life raft tethered nearby suffered a similar splintering fate. And a starboard lifeboat was quickly crunched between the ship's red hull and the icy stone of the north pier.

Humble had been so sure all two dozen crewmembers would ride those lifeboats to safety. They were the best lifeboats built, and the raft was solid, too. He would have launched the crew and let the current and waves throw them to the waiting throngs on the shore. Now, the lifeboats were kindling, flotsam tossing in the surf. The raft wound up on the pier. An uneasy queasiness swept through the captain.

The *Mataafa*'s funnel quit spewing black smoke after the engines died. The clear air was a bit of a relief. But the distress signals honked away. In her newspaper column, Mary McFadden described it this way: "Her great whistles seeming, to the tensely keyed watchers, to speak in alternate accents of frenzied entreaty and despair."

Half of Humble's crew waited in the rear of the steamer. The engines were out. The rudder had been knocked loose. And the boat was breaking in half at the eighth hatch. Humble ordered the men to lower both anchors. But the one on the side that had been striking the pier failed to drop. And the port anchor sank 40 fathoms, or roughly 250 feet of chain, which dragged instead of catching on the lake bottom.

The currents and waves swung the *Mataafa* clear around until the bow pointed northwest toward downtown Duluth, one hundred feet off the north pier. The stern snagged on the stone cribbing of the old piers on the lake bottom. The *Mataafa* had grounded 700 feet from the beach. And the waves kept sweeping over the long deck, which ran some 250 feet between the pilot house up front and the rear quarters below the smokestack. The forecastle windows had been busted out, the gangways were flooded with three feet of water, and doors and hatches had caved in.

Humble started to go aft to tell Bill Most, his engineer, to fill the ballast tanks with water to reduce the pounding. He could get no farther than midship. He ordered the dozen men up front to don their life preservers and stay in shelter so they wouldn't get washed overboard. Then Humble grabbed a megaphone and sang out to somebody—anybody—on shore to send in the lifesavers.

III

"Those waves just strung me out from the rail and
flapped me, but I just had to go and I reckon I am
right glad I did now."

~ Porter Fred Saunders, Amherstburg, Ontario
November 29, 1905

The *Mataafa* cracked at Hatch No. 8, dropping the stern at a slight angle. Those watching from shore saw a fissure in the steamer's lee-ward bulwarks. If there had been any doubt, the next wave gushed red from the iron ore in the cargo hold. A bleeding, harpooned whale would not look much different.

Joe Normandy, a salesman for the Duluth Ice and Fuel Company, lived on the Wieland Flats along the harbor and was watching from shore when the big boat struck. As the steamer started whipping around, Normandy caught a glimpse of four men in the back. He watched one make the leap toward the pier, missing and disappear-ing into the lake. A monstrous wave swept over the tail of the *Mataafa*. After it broke, Normandy couldn't see the other three men. He hoped they hadn't been washed out into the lake, now oozing with red.

The *Mataafa*'s silver smokestack bent back toward the stern, like a man falling backward after losing a high-noon gun duel. The waves, which appeared to freeze as they fell, drenched the men over and over. Beached and pointing northwesterly, the steamer's starboard side was blasted. The men in the stern huddled below deck for thirty minutes. They were dry down there. But then the gangway gave way and water poured in. With the stern leaning low behind the crack, the rear quarters filled with lake water, dousing the fires in the boiler room and forcing the men up to the after deck and smack dab into the brunt of the waves with scant protection from the smokestack or ventilator tubes.

That's why Carl Carlson, a fireman from Chicago, made a jump for the pier. He felt he had nothing to lose. James Early, the new father from Buffalo, had something to lose. He watched Carlson jump. And drown. He wouldn't take the risk. But he had gone to the brink of leaping. And that was enough to put him in danger. Early stood at the stern rail, so close to the pier for which Carlson jumped. He stood between Bill Gilchrist, an oiler from Ontario, and another assistant engineer, C. A. Farenger, from Cleveland.

One moment, they were there. Joe Normandy saw them from the beach, standing together, so close to Duluth's north pier. The next moment, Normandy couldn't see them. He would watch for them as darkness fell that Tuesday. But he wouldn't see them reappear.

The spectators on shore, especially those with marine glasses, could see the huddled sailors in the lee of the smokestack, shivering in cork-filled life jackets for nearly an hour. Thousands along the beach and behind the office windows whispered about the various options. Only seven hundred feet away, the men on the *Mataafa*'s stern debated the same points. It had been nearly an hour, and the boat was increasingly being cleaved into two distinct scenarios: Humble and half his crew up front and the other dozen men huddled by the bent smokestack, exposed to the frigid spray and paralyzing waves.

Second Mate Herbert Emigh could take it no more. He was used to being up front with Captain Humble and First Mate Brown. He'd only come back to untether the barge line. He wanted to get back to the forecastle where he belonged. He had endured enough freezing waves and heard enough muttering from the oilers and firemen. As they argued about what to do, Emigh decided the time to talk was over.

"I'm going up forward, boys," Emigh said, intent on proving it was possible. He meant to inspire them to follow him up the 250-foot gauntlet to the shelter of the pilot house up front.

Fireman Charlie Byrne came from Detroit, seventy miles south of Emigh's home in Lexington Heights, Michigan, along Lake Huron. Captain Humble was a Lexington boy himself. Michiganders stayed together. Byrne nodded and stepped forward behind Emigh. So did Fred Saunders, the plucky porter. He tried to convince the other two black sailors aboard—Walter Bush the cook and Henry Wright the steward—that getting to the forepeak was their best hope. They shook their heads, a frightful stare in their eyes. And their fear was certainly justified.

The waves were crashing across the boat, every few seconds it seemed, washing over and flooding the *Mataafa*'s spar deck with up to ten feet of icy water. Bush and Wright huddled together behind the smokestack. Saunders finally shrugged and joined Emigh and Byrne at the foot of the ladder leading to the deck.

So did Thomas Woodgate, the mass of muscles from Toronto, who had hired on only a week ago in Conneaut. The letter in his pocket, from his father, offered a different outlook: "I am exercising patience until the time arrives and you reach the port. . . ."

Unlike the Old Man in Toronto, Thomas Woodgate, Herbert Emigh, Charlie Byrne, and little Freddie Saunders had exercised enough patience. They were ready to act. Emigh watched the waves, learning their rhythm. Driftwood and wreckage, riding the waves, crashed over the deck and gave Emigh pause. He didn't want to get bashed in the head by a floating chunk of wood. He watched the waves for five minutes.

Then, just as one receded, he bolted, squatting on all fours. He managed to move up a couple hatches, steadying himself on the hatch coamings that held the wooden covers in place. When the boat tossed,

Emigh grabbed hold of the wire railing side line, ducking his head for cover just before a wave struck.

Emigh held on and shook the numbness from his chilled body in shivering spasms. He crawled on, counting to himself the seconds before the next drenching wave would try to drown him. He braced himself against the hatch covers.

Wally Brown, the first mate from Detroit, shouted from the foredeck for Emigh to go back. He waved at him to retreat. After all, the aft quarters were sound and there was fire in the boiler room—or so those up front thought. They didn't realize it had been doused when the starboard gangway gave way and flooded.

Brown and most of the others up front thought Emigh was foolish to take such a risk. They were only seven hundred feet offshore. Certainly the lifesaving crew would send a yawl as a lifeboat or fire a line to rig up a breeches buoy to ferry the men in a rope chair ashore. Brown estimated the men aft would have to dash 250 feet from the smokestack to get up front to the shelter where he stood. Why take a chance of being washed over when patience seemed the soundest strategy?

It wasn't surprising that Brown's perspective differed from that of the men in the rear. Up front, the vessel set up higher than the stern, less exposed to the breaking waves and icy spray.

Emigh timed the waves and clung like a scared cat, claws clutching the wire. Four times, he was drenched, only to scamper up between soaks. When he finally reached Hatch No. 2, Wally Brown was there to grab him with a hug, dragging him by the armpits of his great coat to shelter.

Emigh paused before ducking through the door into the pilot house. He lifted his right arm and curled it, signaling and beckoning the men in the back to follow. He'd shown them he was right. The risk was worth taking. The 250-foot run from aft to fore was possible. You

One of the four sailors in the rear of the *Mataafa* makes his run up the rail toward safety in the forecastle. *Photo by Hugh McKenzie, Lake Superior Maritime Collections, UW–Superior*

just had to hold on for dear life an instant before the waves paralyzed you with a deep chill.

Fred Saunders, the little porter, saw Emigh's hooked arm waving him forward. He made his move, the second crewmember to dash between the splashes of Lake Superior's waves. Saunders had counted the four waves that struck the second mate as he ran the frozen gauntlet. Saunders was ready. With each wave, he braced himself against the bulwarks and squeezed the wire of the rail with both hands.

Four times the waves swept Fred Saunders' feet from under him, flapping him out before throwing him back on deck. Three times, he thought he would die and be washed away in the churning water. But he knew he had to get forward and slipped and slid his way up to the shelter of the pilot house.

The throng cheered from the piers and beach, where more bonfires were being lit. It was after three o'clock in the afternoon and already the short, late-autumn day was darkening. In the faint light, the crowds could see Thomas Woodgate, the brawny coal shoveler from Toronto. He would become the third member of the *Mataafa* crew to make the dash.

"I have dared to presume that you are safe and sound," read the letter in his pocket, from his father.

Three huge waves swept the deck during Thomas Woodgate's run forward. Each one carried him overboard. But each time, he held tight the wire railing in his massive hands and flexed his muscles, chiseled in steamy boiler rooms the last eight months.

Startled onlookers, mouths agape, watched through marine glasses and squinting eyes as Thomas Woodgate hauled himself back onto the *Mataafa*'s battered deck. After the third wave washed Woodgate overboard, he pulled himself back up and said to himself, "No more." He retreated, looking dazed, as if perhaps his head had struck the steamer's steel plates. He clamored back to the smokestack, limping, head down, protecting himself from the next wave.

Unlike the other men iced to the bone in the back of the *Mataafa*, Thomas Woodgate had tried. When he staggered back to the stern, people on shore shouted: "Noooo." They had gasped all three times he'd pulled himself up out of the lake, his hands choking the wire rail. If only he had the gumption to make one more try.

Old-timers in Duluth and other Great Lakes ports tell tales of the Three Sisters, a trio of wild waves that rise up, wreak havoc, and vanish. They've been said to haunt the Inland Seas for centuries. The first sister is large. The next one climbs even higher. The third sister is said to grow three times as monstrous. Thomas Woodgate had fluttered between life and death three times. He would try no more. He would "exercise patience," as his father said in his letter.

Charlie Byrne, the fireman, cheered Woodgate and ran to greet him a few hatches up the deck. Woodgate didn't answer. He just stared and shuffled back. Byrne counted the time between the waves and made his way up the wire railing. It was like walking through a flash flood. He couldn't see a thing. The red, iron-stained water was everywhere. But he got through, like Emigh and Saunders, to the sheltered rooms of the first mate and Captain Humble up front, where the *Mataafa* sat higher and safer in the water.

Humble wondered why the men had waited so long to make their runs. He wished they were all together in the bow. He hated that his crew was separated. Before the four men had made their runs, Humble had attempted to get aft. That's why he wanted his engineer to fill the hold with water, to lessen the pounding the steamer was taking. But Humble had only made it halfway back.

His boat was cut in two. Fifteen men were now up front, cut off by the wash of waves from nine men in the back. Bill Most, the engineer, made a sally to the foot of the ladder planted on the afterdeck. But he watched the waves, crashing almost nonstop, and turned back to join the men trapped and exposed on the rear end of the *Mataafa*.

IV

"Send life savers in a hurry"

> ~ Message scrawled on a board by one of the
> *Mataafa's* crew, thrown out and secured
> by a sailor, who waded into the surf
> November 28, 1905

The *R. W. England* had been pushed two miles south of the canal shortly after one o'clock Tuesday afternoon. By the time Fred Cosford dashed up the beach to alert the U.S. Life-Saving Service, it was about two o'clock. At 2:15 that afternoon, as the lifesavers hauled their apparatus over the debris-riddled beach, pushing south to the stranded *England*, the *Mataafa* was slamming into Duluth's north pier.

The timing could not have been worse. The lifesaving crew had responded promptly, but the *England* wasn't in nearly as dire a circumstance as the *Mataafa*. Yet the surfmen trained and equipped to aid troubled freighters were now miles out of position to help the needier vessel.

The gap in time between the *Mataafa* striking the pier and the lifesaving crew returning to help would last two hours and forty-five minutes. That long stretch was interrupted only briefly by the dramatic runs forward by Emigh, Saunders, Woodgate, and Byrne. The rest of the long wait was excruciating.

Captain Dick Humble simply couldn't understand the lifesavers' absence. His men were freezing. Shore was in sight. Where could the lifesavers possibly be? Humble ventured out from the shelter of the forecastle and shouted through his conical megaphone: "Where are the lifesavers?"

Humble recognized someone on shore, W. W. Waterson of the Pittsburgh Steamship Company, yelling back through his own megaphone. But he couldn't hear the response over the wind and the splash of the waves. So Humble ordered everyone to strap on life jackets. He tightened his own and retreated to his cabin, high aloft the forecastle.

Reaching beneath his bed, Humble pulled out a large drawer and dumped out the few items of clothing that he hadn't put on beneath his great coat. He then carefully tied two ropes to the drawer. One was the lead line, which he would fasten to his deck. The other was a loose heaving line that someone on shore would grab when the drawer drifted close enough on the waves. Then, Humble hoped, they would tie on two lines of their own. He would haul them back and start assembling a breeches buoy, a chair-like pulley rig that would carry the sailors down the two lines to the safety of the shore.

Humble flung the drawer overboard into the heaving lake. When it drifted ashore, the rescue could commence. But the waves quickly smashed the drawer into pieces. Humble exhaled, a puff of steam streaming from his nostrils, and pulled in the two lines. This time, he tied them to a door from the passage room, which he wrenched off its hinges. He tossed the door over the *Mataafa*'s edge and grabbed his megaphone: "Get the door. It's got a line." The door tossed and sank and danced on white-tipped waves. Humble waited and waited until Waterson hollered back through his megaphone. They couldn't retrieve the door.

Hand over hand, Humble pulled the door back. On his third attempt, he lashed another drawer onto the large door and tossed them overboard together. Again, they drifted toward shore, floated back toward the boat—back and forth—for what seemed more like an hour than the minutes that transpired.

Finally, Humble heard them holler from shore: "We got it!" He pumped his fist and allowed a gush of optimism to flow again through his shivering body. He was sure they had tied on their own line and had ordered him to haul away. But when he did, the lines parted, possibly torn by the fangs of sharp rocks or old pier cribbing below the surface. All Humble pulled back was his own line.

Darkness began to blanket Duluth. The crowds didn't wane but swelled to an estimated ten thousand people. Roughly one of every six Duluth residents had found their way to the shore. Some wept. Others offered help. Most gawked. More and more bonfires were lit. They warmed the onlookers, casting eerie glows upon the pale, anguished, and curious faces.

In addition to providing warmth as the temperature dropped below zero, the fires were lit to help ship captains caught out on the lake, offering beacons of hope. For the *Mataafa* crew, less than eight hundred feet away, the fires teased the frozen men. The warmth they so craved was near, yet out of reach.

The fires reflected off Lake Superior's slate water, flashing outlines of the stricken steamer. The firelight bounced off white crests of breaking waves and cast a glow on the *Mataafa*, which separated the gray water from the blackening night sky.

The men of the lifesaving service, under the leadership of Murdoch McLennan, had performed their duties with aplomb down the sandy point. They succeeded in shooting a line to the *R. W. England* and removing nine members of its crew, including the captain. The other dozen men chose to stay on the *England*. McLennan decided not to haul in his lines as long as men were still on board the *England*. He took pride in his crew's service. He planned to stand by until the boat's captain returned and then help remove all the men safely.

Just then, a messenger arrived at the scene, out of breath, eyes bulging. He described to McLennan how the *Mataafa* had struck the north pier, swung around, and cracked some seven hundred feet off shore, just north of the chutes. Some men had dashed up front, the messenger reported. Some might have washed overboard. There was light in the forecastle.

McLennan and five surfmen grabbed shovels and lanterns and a No. 4 and a No. 9 shot line. They hustled back to their station, hauled their apparatus cart to the government warehouse pier, hopped on a tugboat, and zipped at full throttle across the harbor to Singer's Dock. The *Mataafa* lay about a thousand feet away.

The beach was rugged and the surf relentless. Three lifesavers had been left at the government pier in all the hurry. They scrounged up extra shot lines as the tug circled back to fetch them. The ferrying took nearly a half hour, but the lifesavers were in place on the cramped, rocky beach. It was five o'clock and growing darker.

Of course, a lifeboat would offer the best chance to rescue the sailors. But none was available. Even if there had been a yawl, launching into the backlashing waves off the pier, into the cold darkness, would have been suicidal.

McLennan pushed thoughts of a lifeboat out of his mind. He would try the Lyle gun and prepare to wait out the night until the sea died down and light returned with the dawn. The Lyle gun was like a small cannon that rocketed lifelines to stranded swimmers or, as in this case, steamers. It had worked like a charm that very afternoon at the scene of the beached *England*.

Humble hollered through his megaphone to shoot the line aft, where the men were in the greatest danger. McLennan's men positioned the gun and fired a No. 7 and a No. 9 line. They landed amidships on the deck, now a wall of icy Lake Superior water dividing the men in the forecastle from what was left of the men aft.

From the forecastle, Captain Humble watched the first two shot lines fly across the middle of the *Mataafa*'s deck, impossible to retrieve. Humble lifted his megaphone and told them to fire forward of the foremast or back to the smokestack.

To work properly, a breeches buoy required two lines: a lead and haul whip. When the lifesavers drew back the lines fired from the Lyle gun, they found the lines had parted near the wreck. So they hauled the Lyle gun to a different position, windward and straight across the water from the bow. A third line, a No. 9, was fired and sailed across the pilot house. The crowds circling the bonfires unleashed a jubilant cheer. After hours of anxious fretting, they danced and shouted hysterically.

Humble watched the third line, fired from a new position, soar right toward him. First Mate Wally Brown and watchman Grantley West patted Humble on the back as they went out to retrieve the line. Fighting numb fingers and drenching spray, Humble tried to untangle the shot line and the trail line, which had frozen together. Separating the lines was crucial—and impossible. So Humble pulled out his knife and cut the shot line. Wally Brown and Grantley West then scrambled up the riggings aloft, intent on fastening the line to the main spar. Every few minutes, a wave would wash over them,

Mataafa First Mate Wally Brown (*left*) poses next to an unknown man in 1904. *J. W. Westcott Co. Archives*

snatching their breath. With no feeling left in their hands, there was no way to tie the line to the mast.

Humble barked through his megaphone, telling Brown to try tying up to the shroud of the rigging instead. This worked. Brown and West stumbled down to the deck, nearly too frozen to move. Humble dragged them by the armpits of their wet great coats, pulling them into the wheelhouse's shelter. Theirs hands and feet had turned into stumps of ice. They shivered on the floor, flapping like fish on the bottom of an angler's boat.

Humble turned his megaphone toward shore and shouted that the tail block had been tied fast to the rigging. On shore, hundreds of hands reached for the rope. Police tried to keep the crowd back, but everyone was determined to help the lifesavers tugging the line, linking them to the marooned crew.

But twists and turns gnarled the line. Within minutes, the pliable rope had turned into a solid mass of ice. On the beach, the lifesavers were so cramped they couldn't keep the two parts of the whip separated. The twisted lines dropped into the water's strong undertow. Just as the lifesavers cleared one tangle, the whip chafed on the rocky bottom and severed.

Rigging a breeches buoy now seemed futile. The cold crippled both rope and hand. Lifesavers pulled in their third shot line—the one that seemingly had been tied fast to the *Mataafa*'s shroud. Then they fired a fourth attempt from the Lyle gun. It seemed like a direct hit, landing near the foremast. They signaled the *Mataafa*'s crew, repeatedly, to haul away. But they received no response from the cracked freighter.

In the darkness, Humble, Brown, and West didn't realize the tail block on the fourth line had shot through a busted pilot house window into a lamp room. Now all Humble had at his disposal were his megaphone, his vocal cords, and his lungs. Weakened by hunger, thirst, and exposure—and his men freezing—Humble hollered: "Can't you do anything for us?"

He begged them to launch a lifeboat. Humble could barely hear the men ashore yelling back. The noise of the storm drowned out any communication or, worse yet, twisted it into tragic miscommunication. Waterson, the Pittsburgh Steamship agent who shouted through his own megaphone, thought Captain Humble had said: "All men forward." In reality, Humble had screamed: "The ones forward are all right, but we fear the ones aft are in danger."

From five o'clock to ten o'clock, Humble and Waterson had frantically tried to use the megaphones to instigate a rescue. None of it had worked.

Dejected, Humble told his men to turn in for the long night ahead.

V

"Despair simply froze our blood when the darkness came."

~ Deckhand Harry Larson of Superior, Wisconsin

Captain Humble gave up any notion of securing a line and rigging a breeches buoy. He had screamed through his megaphone until his throat was raw.

On shore, Mary McFadden knew her deadline was approaching. Yet she stood hypnotized on an overlook some thousand feet from the *Mataafa*, now cracked and groaning. She knew she had to get back to the *News Tribune* office to type up her report. Between the

Waves pound the *Mataafa*. *Great Lakes Marine Collection of the Milwaukee Public Library/Wisconsin Marine Historical Society*

wind and waves, she could only hear bits of what the captain yelled through his megaphone. The last three words she heard that night came out clear before drowning in the noise: "My God, can't. . . ."

From the weather station on the first floor of his house on the hill, Herbert Richardson examined his graph paper and shook his head. He'd never seen anything like it. For thirteen hours, his record-keeping equipment showed the rate of the wind had been sixty miles per hour with a maximum rate for any five minutes of sixty-eight miles per hour. No other storm he'd witnessed had ever approached this one for relentless continuity.

The *Mataafa's* drama played out only seven hundred feet from the shore of Duluth. *Photo by Hugh McKenzie, Lake Superior Maritime Collections, UW–Superior*

In the forecastle of the *Mataafa*, Captain Humble prepared his men for a long night. Getting to the lamp room was impossible, with doors, windows, and wreckage blocking the access. Humble ordered the men to light what lamps they could find, and he collected all the dry blankets: "Wrap them around your shoulders."

All the rooms in the foredeck were flooded, so the fifteen men up front climbed into Captain Humble's cabin. The lamps cast their faces in an eerie, yellow glow, and the smell of kerosene filled the cramped quarters. The glass porthole windows had shattered early in the game. And the doors were gone, either torn off by the seas or wrenched off when Humble tried to send them adrift with the drawer from beneath his bed. That had been the first failed attempt to establish a link with the people on shore.

Ernest Dietz, a deckhand from Winnipeg, grabbed an icicle from the top of a window frame. With the drinking-water tanks located in the stern, few men had risked a run back to quench their thirsts for many hours. So icicles, which hung from all the windows and doorways, had to sustain them. The instant Dietz pulled off one of the frozen daggers to suck out the lake water, another icicle formed in its place almost immediately.

Wally Brown, the first mate, was more drenched than most of the men after his trip on deck to tie the split line to the rigging shroud. As he shivered, Brown couldn't help but chuckle. The men looked like a tribe of Indians in the glow of a ritual fire. Wrapped in blankets, they began to dance around in Indian fashion, clapping their arms. The slap of men's hands on each others' shoulders served as the drumbeat.

Humble, his mates Brown and Emigh, and wheelman James Hatch made it their charge to keep the men dancing. "Everyone, on your feet!" they hollered. Exhaustion and bitter cold tempted each one to collapse in a heap. Sleep tantalized the men. But each knew sleep would be deadly.

So as wave after wave crashed through windows and doorways, the fifteen men in the captain's cabin of the *Mataafa* rushed from one side of the room to the next, trying to avoid the ice bath that rolled over the stragglers. Dodging the waves kept their circulation going. And the icicles kept their thirst at bay.

At two in the morning, the crowds on shore watched in silence as the lamp lights in the pilot house began to fade. Captain McLennan's lifesaving crew had been ordered to catch some rest at midnight. But many men and women remained on the beach, stoking the bonfires with driftwood. Watching and waiting.

Mary McFadden returned to her newspaper office to write:

A noble lake leviathan, the *Mataafa*, is lying just off the canal pier with the fate of her crew unknown, while watchers are pacing up and down besides the bonfires on shore and waiting for daylight.

Another boat is being broken to pieces by the angry seas near Lakewood, but her crew is safe and sound. Still another is beached above the canal, her crew is safe with friends. What more despoliation and tragedy awaits this morning's knowledge cannot now be guessed. Science and human endeavor and the mighty work of human hands were flouted all day and all night by the elements gone mad.

The monotony and the cold, meanwhile, had frozen the *Mataafa*'s crew into a kind of comatose state between life and death. When Wally Brown saw Harry Larson's head start to bob, he shook him awake. Shivering, Larson was so tempted to surrender to deadly sleep. Captain Humble himself smacked Larson's shoulders to jostle him back among the living.

This went on for hours after the lamps started to sputter, hiss, and go dark. The men dashed back and forth. They danced in slow motion as glints of bonfire light reflected off the choppy water of Lake Superior. The pounding of hands filled the silence with deep thuds and claps. The smell of bonfire smoke wafted out to them from shore.

At three o'clock in the morning, when most of the lamp lights had dimmed, Humble became convinced of his next decision. It was getting colder. His crew would freeze to death before daybreak. He must act. It was his last hope.

Returning to Duluth. Sailing past Two Harbors. Severing his tie with the barge. Trying to shoot the chutes. Sending off drawers and doors and waiting for a lifeboat or a lifeline. Humble second-guessed none of these decisions. All night long, he'd convinced himself that other Great Lakes masters would have made the same choices. But none of them had worked.

He had to do something more. So Captain Dick Humble waded into the water sloshing through the hallways below the *Mataafa*'s deck. The water was three feet deep, sludge-like, and partially frozen with a thin, glassy layer caking the surface.

Humble trudged into the windlass room and found a jar of kerosene in a cupboard, which held a few rags and dry matchsticks. He grabbed a hatchet and chopped some wooden molding from the adjacent bathroom. With whatever splinters and scrap wood he could gather, Humble ignited a small fire in the bathtub.

Outside, the predawn blackness eased into gray. And the sea had finally calmed to the point that only a few inches of water sloshed over the deck of the windlass room. Earlier in the night, the water level where Humble now stood had been two feet deep.

Humble called all hands down to the fire. His voice was raspy, wasted on shouts through the megaphone. The men splashed through waist-high water in the hallway until all fifteen surrounded the blazing bathtub. Their clothes, heavy and frigid, began to thaw. Humble and the men added wood and kerosene to the fire until seven-thirty Wednesday morning. At that point, someone went out on the deck and reported back that the lifesaving crew had launched a boat. They were coming, at last.

VI

"There is one prayer in the heart of every Duluthian,
one hope against hope—that the heroic crew of the
Mataafa *may, by some miracle, be brought back*
whole and safe to shore with daylight this morning,
and that the wreckage that will strew the lakeshore
from Minnesota Point to Lakewood may not include
anything inanimate that was once human."

~ Mary McFadden, *Duluth News Tribune*
November 29, 1905

Snow covered the stone buildings, muddy streets, and iced sidewalks of downtown Duluth that Wednesday morning. Already, Dunkan and Crawford's morgue on Second Avenue was busy. Up the hill and four blocks east, the morticians at John Flood and Daniel Horgan's morgue were preparing for a busy day-before-Thanksgiving as well. Two bodies had washed up on shore: one late last night and one this morning. They were shuttled to the two morgues.

The skeletal remains of a headless, armless torso had turned up on the beach so late that they weren't recovered until morning light. The lifesaving crew had taken its rest and the waves were still smashing the shore with such an unpredictable wrath, it was agreed that waiting until daybreak made the most sense.

Most of the flesh was gone from the bones of the torso, which was pinned to the surf by a heavy chunk of weathered wood. It looked like driftwood but likely was an old spar. Whoever's skeleton this was, he had likely lashed himself to the mast. His body was taken by horse-drawn hearse to Durkan and Crawford's morgue a few doors down from Superior Street, the spine of downtown Duluth's commerce district.

The undertakers quickly determined that the body, shrouded in waterlogged pale pink flesh, had not come off the *Mataafa* or any other vessel caught in this storm. It must have been a sailor from the whaleback steamer *Wilson* that collided with the *Hadley* more than three years earlier. The bay had never given up the dead from that wreck. Among the lost was the cook named Tripp from Collingwood, Ontario. He'd gone under while treading water with Arthur Daggett, another Lake Huron kid.

Bill Lanigan's bar and restaurant sat just one block west of Durkan and Crawford's morgue, across Third Avenue. The saloon started filling up with shipwrecked and storm-stunned sailors, captains, and mates early that Wednesday. They'd come off the *Crescent City*, *England*, and *Arizona* and eventually would pour into Duluth from the *Lafayette*, *Manila*, *Spencer*, *Amboy*, and *Madeira*.

Sixty of the glazed-eyed seamen found rooms at the sumptuous St. Louis Hotel, many sharing two to a bed. Others found warm quilts and mattresses in smaller inns. Many of the seamen found their way to Lanigan's. As did the newspapermen and the one woman in their ilk: Mary McFadden of the *Duluth News Tribune*.

The chatter drowned out the sound of clinking mugs and clanging plates of warm bread and crocks of stew. Among the patrons was Arthur Daggett, the watchman from Collingwood, Ontario, recently off the *Crescent City*. He was in a cantankerous mood.

Daggett had overheard a shore captain going on about what a snap it had been for the crew of the *Crescent City* to get off the steamer on the rocky shore near Lakewood. A fight nearly broke out and the verbose fellow, wisely, left the tavern.

"The man talked like an imbecile," Daggett fumed.

A group of reporters circled Daggett's end of the table, which was crowded with steaming bowls and beer mugs.

"Snap! I wish I had that man out there with us and he would see what a snap we had."

Daggett praised his capable master, *Crescent City* Captain Frank Rice, who had not lost a single life when his steamer crashed ashore.

"He knows what a snap is on the Lakes when he sees one," Daggett said to no one in particular. "And he didn't think that shore was a snap when we went up against it."

Between gulps of ale, Daggett recalled how Captain Rice had gathered all the *Crescent City* crew around him on the forward deck to offer a prayer for their souls. "He realized that the chances for any of us getting off were slight."

Daggett paused to let the drama build. His storytelling talent was as honed as his swimming ability. And that had come in handy when the schooner sank below him on Lake Michigan—and when he jumped from the sinking *Wilson* in 1902 and treaded water for nearly an hour before a tug came for him.

The reporters, sailors, and barmaids leaned in to hear Daggett recount his exploits. Lightning had struck him thrice, if you will. He meandered around before building to the climax of the *Crescent City's* tale. Mary McFadden jotted it all down in her notebook.

"Just then Providence stepped in and threw the boat stern up against the shore. This, ordinarily, would have made matters worse," Daggett explained.

"But she struck there and didn't slide back and pound as would generally be the sure case."

Arthur Daggett shook his head, topped with tousled hair. "That man made me tired with his talk of a snap."

It didn't take long for word of the headless, armless torso at Durkan and Crawford's morgue to drift one block down Superior Street and into the hubbub of Lanigan's. Daggett suddenly grew quiet.

He remembered the jolt that woke him from a deep sleep in his quarters below the *Wilson*'s arched, whaleback deck. They were a half-mile off the piers of the Duluth Ship Canal by the time Daggett scrambled to the deck. And they were sinking fast.

Daggett and Tripp, the cook who grew up with him in Collingwood, looked at each other, nodded, and jumped together before the *Wilson* took its last plunge. They bobbed in the calm, cold lake waves about ten feet apart, yelling in unison for help. Twice, they dropped below the surface of Lake Superior. Despite their exhaustion, they came up to gulp for air and scream some more.

The third time Daggett went under, he came up alone. He searched for Tripp but never saw him again. No one did. Now, three years later, Daggett sat in the chaos of Lanigan's and felt paralyzed. His heart seemed to constrict in his chest. Could the skeleton in the morgue down the block be the bones of Tripp?

Crowds started to gather early that Wednesday at Flood and Horgan's morgue just up the hill and four blocks east. The curious, the grief-wrenched, and the gawkers.

The first body arrived with no shoes or trousers, only a flannel shirt, woolen mittens, and heavy underclothing. He must have divested himself of his shoes and pants to facilitate a swim for shore, undertaker John Flood surmised. This body must be that of the sailor rumored to have jumped for the north pier after the *Mataafa* struck, spun, and cracked within a hundred feet of the stone pier head.

Joe Normandy, the ice salesman from Wieland Flats, told the story of the man's failed jump for the north pier. The dead man's face was badly bruised, and his nose and lips had swelled, disfiguring an otherwise chiseled, handsome Scandinavian face. Mortician Daniel Horgan speculated that the man had probably tried to cling to the boat after his unsuccessful leap, only to get thrown against the ship. The undertakers debated whether the blows to his face had come before he drowned or visa versa.

Before long, onlookers came forward and identified the corpse in the flannel shirt. He was Carl Carlson, an oiler from Chicago. He'd shipped on the *Mataafa* in Superior, making his familiar face easy to identify despite the problems with his nose and lips. Preparations were made to send Carlson's remains to his sister in Chicago.

VII

"*As the gray light broke around the wreck of the* Mataafa *yesterday morning the question on the lips of weary watchers who had kept the bonfires going through the darkness was 'how many are still alive?'*"

~ Mary McFadden, *Duluth News Tribune*
November 30, 1905

The people of Duluth returned to the beach Wednesday morning. Men and women alike, having crammed the waterfront until midnight, now fixed their gaze on a light illuminating from a porthole window on the *Mataafa*. Encased in ice from the tip of its masts, the giant ore ship sat cracked seven hundred feet off shore.

Captain Murdoch McLennan of the lifesaving service hadn't sat down all night, let alone slept. His six men hadn't rested much easier. By five o'clock in the morning, they were back at their posts. With the help of dozens of onlookers, they carried down two surf boats. McLennan requested a megaphone, which was promptly brought down. He yelled out repeatedly to the *Mataafa*.

When Captain Dick Humble stepped out the door of his battered quarters, a booming cheer rang out from shore. Humble lifted his megaphone and shouted back: "All alive forward. Can you get us ashore?"

But Lake Superior was heaving again by eight o'clock and Murdoch delayed the launching of the surf boat. The whispering on shore was growing louder, and the criticism of his lifesaving crew started to rain down in verbal pelts that stung McLennan like the icy snow. Many people were calling him incompetent and pestering him to send out the boat. He knew he could wait no more.

Facing the crashing waters, McLennan ordered his six lifesavers onto the surf boat. Dozens of men stepped forward, hands on the gunnel and boots in the iced water. They shoved the boat into the breakers, which once again were rolling over the deck of the *Mataafa*. White spray, like a thundercloud, blasted the broken ore boat. Ice had wrapped itself around the riggings and masts, frosting everything in a glassy crystal.

Cheers arose each time the lifesaving boat breasted the breakers. The nose of the thirty-foot wooden yawl boat pointed straight up toward the sky one instant, and then straight down the backside of a wave the next. McLennan, wearing a boxy hat, stood tall in the back of the tossing lifeboat, his hand on the long rudder oar that he used to steer. His men rowed, facing the shore, their backs toward the wreck, pulling with all their strength.

McLennan wished the seas had calmed. The last thing he needed now was to capsize. Finally, he reached the steel-sided freighter and a rope was tossed up to the pleading hands of the *Mataafa* crew.

Lifesavers rescued the survivors off the *Mataafa* on November 29, 1905.
Historical Collections of the Great Lakes, Bowling Green State University

Someone on deck grabbed the rope, and the onlookers clapped with mittened applause.

The rope was fastened, and Humble called out seven names. McClure. Dietz. Byrne. Saunders. Hatch. Yake. Carlson. With the drenching waves and spray as high as the mast-top, nature spelled chaos on the deck. But the men moved with deliberation and order, as if performing an oft-repeated ritual march. When Captain Humble called each name, the man stepped forward, bent over, and crawled to the steamer's rail. The captain and first mate helped each sailor grab hold of the rope.

The crowds now stood silent as stones. The tumultuous seas were threatening to capsize McLennan's lifeboat. He looked up, fearing the worst: that the first sailor would drop from the frozen rope into the black water. The rope swayed so much, McLennan worried that the men would be banged senseless against the *Mataafa*'s steel shell.

Each man paused before rising from the crawling position. Then with resolution and commitment, he grabbed the rope, snaked it around his legs, and lowered himself to the rocking boat below. After the seventh one had slipped down the iced line and into the arms of the lifesavers, McLennan judged the boat full and ordered his men to row the shivering crewmembers ashore. First, though, they sent up a basket with lunch and a bottle of brandy.

Three of the rescued men were carried to the ambulance wagon, including McClure, the wheelman, whose hands had been cut and bloodied by the shattered glass of the forecastle windows. Blood and ice caked his forearms. The others walked, half carried by the onlookers, to waiting carriages. At a trot, they were zipped up Superior Street to the St. Louis Hotel. Onlookers crowded around the carriages to get a close look at the frozen sailors as they made their way up to warm rooms.

The St. Louis Hotel in Duluth is where *Mataafa* crew recovered with warm whiskey and thick blankets. *Courtesy of the* Minneapolis Star Tribune *library*

In Room 304, deckhand Leon Yake of Michigan sat in a wingchair next to Ernest Dietz, the watchman from Winnipeg. Both men, in their young twenties, smoked fat cigars and slurped hot whiskeys to unwind before napping. They'd hadn't changed out of their filthy, damp clothes. The two men smiled and laughed one second and sat stunned and contemplative the next.

Across the hall, Fred Saunders, the black porter who'd made the dash from stern to safety, sat up in one bed. Fireman Charlie Byrne, who'd also run the icy gauntlet, was there, too. Watchman James Hatch, in a bed next to Saunders, munched on a sandwich of thick bread and roasted beef and sipped a hot whiskey. The men hadn't eaten since lunch at noon on Tuesday, more than twenty-four hours ago.

A newspaperman knocked on their door and was let in. Mary McFadden wormed her way up the stairs, too.

Hatch was from Winnipeg, but he had shipped out of Duluth, so he was well known to the reporters. He shared a bed with Axel Carlson, the fireman from Chicago. Carlson had finished his sandwich and pulled the covers over his head, slowly thawing his frozen body under a mound of thick, woolen blankets. He poked his nose out and added some comments to the recount of the ordeal Hatch was serving up to the reporters.

"We were drenched with spray every time a wave struck us," Axel said. "We were sheltered from the full force of the waves. But the spray would blow over us. If you don't believe it, look at the clothes."

He pointed to a waterlogged mountain of soggy woolen garments in the center of the floor. Back in Room 304, Ernest Dietz had grown quiet next to Yake. The aroma of burnt tobacco from their cigars clouded into a haze above them. He exhaled a puff of smoke and looked at the newspaperman visiting the room.

"We have yet heard nothing from the fellows in the back end. I guess they all perished. It was a dirty shame. They were a nice set of fellows. If you hear anything about them, let us know."

VIII

"The tales of heroic struggle, of the desperate endurance of joy, of rescue, and of the awful roster of the dead were carried over the city from tongue to tongue while thousands gathered to see the first of the survivors landed safely ashore; others to scan the ice-clad protuberances upon the shattered afterdeck, any of which might be a corpse."

~ Mary McFadden, *Duluth News Tribune*
November 30, 1905

As the waves subsided Wednesday morning, the throngs of onlookers descended on the north pier. The footing was slippery, with glaze ice forcing people to mince their tiny steps like penguins. But they kept coming until more than a hundred men and women lined the pier, elbowing for a close look. If they had stones, they could easily pitch them on the *Mataafa*'s icy deck some hundred feet away.

Onboard, Humble opened the basket of warm bread, cheese wedges, and dried meat and passed the bottle of brandy around the fire that still crackled in the forecastle. He didn't even exchange words with Wally Brown, his first mate. Just a glance aft and Brown knew what his master wanted. It was time to go back to the see what had become of the men in the stern. The knots in their stomachs and the ache in their hearts foretold a ghastly scene.

The deck was glazed over with a thin layer of ice, so Dick Humble and Wally Brown took to crawling to the back of the *Mataafa*. They found four men on the port side, facing the beach—frozen to death. They discovered a fifth body, that of deckhand Thomas McCloud, hidden in the leeside ventilator. He had climbed in the large, bent-elbow of thin metal, seeking shelter. He clutched the sides of the tube with woolen mittens. The ventilator was aimed at moving fresh air from the deck through the stale air below. It wasn't meant to protect a man from wind and waves.

The faces on the other corpses on the *Mataafa* were hard to make out. Ice, frost, and death had rendered them unrecognizable. But McCloud's face was all too discernible. He stared through lifeless eyes toward shore, where the flicker of bonfires and even the chatter of conversation had punctuated his last moments.

His mouth was gaping, crying out in silence. He had sought refuge in the bent, steel tube. He thought it would give him another layer of protection from the wind and spray. He held on tight, waiting for daylight. He was little known, having hired on only recently in Conneaut, Ohio. One of his crewmates described him as a roving spirit. He carried a notebook that would tell Flood and Horgan at the morgue that he was Thomas McCloud of Brandenburg, Kentucky.

Humble and Brown crawled along the *Mataafa*'s stern, clinging to lines and rails twisted in the storm. They found Thomas Woodgate in the lee of the smokestack, face up, lying on his back with arms outstretched. He had tried three times to skirt the combers and make it to the forecastle. Each time, he had been washed off the deck. But his arms and shoulders were strong as steel. He'd grabbed the wire fence rail and pulled himself back on board. He'd fought against Lake Superior's attempt to drown him and won. But he was dead nevertheless, killed by wind and cold instead of icy water. The position of his body hinted that he had huddled down as close to the smokestack as he could. When he died, the wind knocked him over backward. His body lay buried under snow and ice. His jacket pocket held the letter from his father, who dared to presume he was safe from stormy weather.

Bill Most, the chief engineer, had in his pocket receipts of registered letters to his wife in Chicago, on 133 Klabble Street. Like Woodgate, Most's arms were outstretched from his attempt to hug the smokestack and deter the wind. But unlike Woodgate, Bill Most was sprawled face down. The side of his skull had been smashed by something, perhaps causing his death, perhaps occurring after the life had frozen out of the engineer's body.

Henry Wright, the steward, also had a massive gash in the back of his head. His body was stuck in a hatchway twenty feet forward of the stack. Encased in ice, Wright's body was twisted and distorted. His right leg was wrenched backward, up toward the wound in his skull. The morticians found card No. 121 of the Marine Cooks and Stewards Union among his clothing. He had paid his December dues.

Humble and Brown crawled back to the forward deck as the surfboat returned, tossing like driftwood in the breakers. Again, Humble and Brown called out the names. Coulter. Yates. Larson. Suttle. West. Emigh. They helped each of the six men twist themselves down the rope to the boat. After Wally Brown slid down, Humble took a glance at the shattered forecastle and gazed down the long deck to the crooked, damaged smokestack and the iced rigging and masts aft. Then Dick Humble lowered himself down the rope to McLennan's surfboat. Several times, they almost capsized during their seven-hundred-foot dash to shore. Onshore, carriages were waiting to take them over to the St. Louis Hotel.

About three o'clock Wednesday afternoon, the lifesaving crew returned to the *Mataafa* with hatchets and iron bars. They would find Walter Bush, the cook, deeply imbedded in ice, trapped beneath a fallen ventilator. His right arm was extended as if he had been holding out his overcoat for protection.

The tugboat *Inman* sputtered out for the bodies. Hours of careful work were required before the frozen men were chipped and chiseled free from the ice. They would thaw at Flood and Horgan's morgue, where thousands of men and women had come to gaze at their bodies. They had cheered the rescues of the *Mataafa*'s fifteen survivors and stood silent as the bodies were removed. Now, they would leave the spectacle that had played out for two days on the waterfront to come face-to-face with the tragedy at the funeral home down Superior Street.

"Nine poor fellows are dead in the stern," Harry Larson, the seaman from Superior, told Mary McFadden as he limped into the horse-drawn hack for a ride to the hotel. "Oh God, it's awful. We knew our nine comrades in the aft part were doomed."

Only six of those nine were found. Carl Carlson had washed ashore in his flannel shirt and woolen mittens. McCloud had hidden in the ventilator. Most and Wright had their heads bashed in. Bush was underneath the knocked-over ventilator. And Woodgate was sprawled on his back, arms wide.

Three bodies were not found: William Gilchrist, the oiler from Ontario; and Bill Most's assistant engineers, C. A. Farenger of Cleveland and James Early—who would never meet his new baby daughter back on 599 Riley Street in Buffalo.

IX

"I did this on my own resolution. I received no orders

from the Pittsburgh Steamship Company, or any of its

employees, of any nature regarding my departure. I

used my own judgment, as I always do in such cases."

~ Notarized statement of Captain Dick Humble

December 1, 1905

Thanksgiving came to Duluth that Thursday with hundreds of stranded sailors drinking heavily. Their lot included the nine crewmembers of the *Nasmyth*, the barge that Captain Humble ordered to drop its towline. It had ridden out the storm, anchors clawing the lake bottom, and all had survived. Humble was sure he was casting the freight boat off into the devil's hands. He would never have guessed the barge would fare better than his steamer, *Mataafa*.

Crowds continued to gather on the piers and at the morgue. Half-sunken and beached freights dotted the shore, from the sand-trapped *England* on Minnesota Point to the *Crescent City* resting in a safe cove five miles north in Lakewood. The *Mataafa*, angled just off the north pier, dominated everyone's gaze and talk.

In the days that followed, sermons were delivered, a diver in a heavy suit and helmet searched the *Mataafa*'s sunken after chambers, and a chartered train spewing black smoke rattled into the Duluth depot. In its plush coach car, cigar smoke exhaled through the pug nose of Harry Coulby, the forty-year-old president of the massive merged fleet of the silver smokestacked Pittsburgh Steamship Company.

From the *Madeira*, which had sunk below the cliffs of Gold Rock, to the *Crescent City* to the *Mataafa*, the storm paralyzed Coulby's Great Lakes armada.

The talk, naturally, turned to blame. Six men on the *Mataafa* were dead. Three were missing. Fifteen were sipping hot whiskeys under quilts on the third floor of the St. Louis Hotel. The whispering turned into arguments, ringing out at Lanigan's pub, on the piers, and in the lines waiting to view the bodies at Flood and Horgan's morgue.

When it came to pointing fingers, people were picking one of four corners. Most of the criticism's sting was felt by Murdoch McLennan, the amiable, bear-sized captain of the U.S. Life-Saving Service in Duluth. *Mataafa* captain Dick Humble assumed as much of the blame as he could. Working people eyed Coulby, the English shipping baron from Cleveland who had busted unions, flexed his muscle for control against the vessel masters, and got rich in the process. Coulby, in turn, laid the responsibility squarely on nature, pure and simple.

And meteorologist Herbert Richardson could only shake his head as he analyzed his graphs and record-keeping apparatus.

The blips and lines of Richardson's equipment told the same tale that all on the waterfront could see plainly with their own eyes. A sixty-foot gash had been torn through the sand bar harbor of Minnesota Point, cutting a wide, shallow new channel. Lighthouses and whistle houses had been wrecked. Timbers and coal were strewn on the piers and docks. Sand cribs that once helped form the breakwater, a hundred feet by eighty feet and thirty feet deep, were now slapped haphazardly on the beach.

At first, Duluth physician John McCuen planned on conducting a formal inquest. He would select one of the six thawing corpses at the morgue and subpoena witnesses. The afternoon newspaper insisted: "An effort will be made to ascertain if any person was to blame for the loss of nine lives."

Around dinnertime before the afternoon inquest, McCuen met with John McClintock, the St. Louis County attorney. After lengthy discussion, the inquest was called off. There were jurisdictional issues.

McClintock pointed to a law passed in 1901, the same year the Pittsburgh Steamship Company's dominant fleet was born. Under McClintock's interpretation of the law, coroners were instructed to investigate only violent deaths. Casualties caused by storms or other natural acts did not require inquests. Never mind that the men on the *Mataafa* couldn't have died more violently. McCuen would not gauge blame. Instead, he signed six death certificates. Each one listed the cause of death as "exposure to cold and waves—shipwreck."

McCuen released the bodies, and John Flood and Daniel Horgan made arrangements with family members. The body of fireman Thomas Woodgate, thirty, was shipped on the South Shore rail to Toronto. Cook Walter Bush, twenty-eight, and steward Henry Wright, forty-five, also went home via the South Shore to Amherstburg, Ontario.

The body of engineer William Most, thirty-six, was sent on the Omaha Road to his wife in Cleveland. Oiler Carl Carlson, twenty-five, was shipped to his sister in Chicago. And McCloud's corpse had the longest trip, to Lexington, Kentucky.

Among the gawkers and spectators at the morgue was the inconsolable William Gilchrist of Wharton, Ontario. He had come to recover the body of his son, William Junior, the other oiler. The father had come on the first train, hoping to both find his son among the survivors and prove the newspapers wrong with their roster of the dead. He paced and sobbed when confronted with the worst possible news. Not only was his son uncounted among the living, but his body was missing, as was the privilege to bring him home for burial.

Along with the young Gilchrist, two others had vanished into the heaving Lake Superior waters, just at the harbor's door: Jim Early, the father from Buffalo, and the other assistant engineer, C. A. Farenger.

William Hoy, one of Duluth's tug masters, was also the city's most experienced deepwater diver. He stepped into his thick, rubberized suit and fastened a belt of weighted bricks as they rode out to the *Mataafa* on the tug *Medina*. Bill Hargraves, his dive tender, came along, and Bill Reed, master of the tin stacker *Mariposa*, took charge of the rescue.

Captain Humble wanted to return to his boat with the diver. But Reed convinced his friend to rest. Dick Humble's nerves were frayed. He had slept little. Consumed by guilt, he'd lost his appetite and ability to rest. The tragedy was literally tearing at his gut.

Reed and Hargraves steadied the long, wooden ladder and kept the air hose from tangling. Hoy descended, carrying seventy extra pounds of bulk, including the heavy iron helmet he gently lowered over his head. The helmet featured a glass window face mask, an air valve, and a collar that fit snugly over his shoulders, not all too different from the knights of King Arthur's era.

Hoy's journey into the sunken after section of the *Mataafa* was delayed at the start by a thin layer of ice, which he needed to shatter with a gaffe. About six feet down the companionway, Hoy found his way to the submerged after quarters. He signaled the tender before dropping into eight feet of cloudy, cold lake water. A sucking, gurgling sound echoed off the steel partitions. With heavy steps, Hoy trudged carefully through the water into the after hallway, making

Although not taken during the 1905 storm, this photo shows a Duluth diving team similar to the one that searched the *Mataafa* after the storm. *Minnesota Historical Society*

sure his air hose didn't twist. With the stick he used to bust through the ice, Hoy probed under bunks and amid debris that had flooded below deck. The storm had left a frozen, underwater chaos. Wet flannel shirts, long johns, and stockings cluttered the floor. Hoy poked them gently with his stick. They fluttered in slow motion like seaweed.

Broken furniture and partitions bobbed near the surface. The powerful waves had twisted and warped the steel stairway. Hoy left the hallway and dropped down another eight feet into the engine and boiler rooms. Up on the tug, Reed and Hargraves cranked the spool and let more air hose go.

Hoy probed with his gaffe around piles of coal and wreckage. Finally, after two hours of checking every cranny and nook, Hoy signaled that he was ready to ascend. Oiler Bill Gilchrist and assistant engineers C. A. Farenger and Jim Early must have washed overboard. Whether before or after their deaths remained unknown.

Mary McFadden waited onshore for the tug to return with the diver and tender. She found herself again in the midst of a large crowd that included some of Duluth's finest women, sketchiest men, and even the Reverend Merton Rice of the First Methodist Episcopal Church.

The onlookers whispered back and forth before letting loose a collective sigh when it was clear the *Medina* was coming back empty-handed. In her *Duluth News Tribune*, McFadden wrote that everyone's hope of finding the three missing bodies "had proved once more a will o' the wisp.

"A sigh of disappointment marked the appearance of the unsuccessful searcher on deck. Nothing of the smallest value was found and the party left the hulk empty handed and disappointed, though the fruition of their hopes would have meant that they bear back a burden of death."

X

"While I have been in Duluth I have heard there was some criticism on the street. . . . I also understand that there have been rumors."

~ Pittsburgh Steamship Company
President Harry Coulby
Thanksgiving, November 30, 1905

Coulby's special train puffed out black smoke as it arrived in Duluth on Wednesday night, some eight hours after the frozen bodies had been hauled off the *Mataafa*. Roaring up the Omaha Road, the five-car train covered the 480 miles from Chicago to Duluth in less than twelve and a half hours. The old record was thirteen hours and forty minutes.

Coulby bounded off his coach car with W. W. Smith, the Pittsburgh Steamship Company's marine superintendent. They made their way to a carriage, which promptly delivered them to the Spaulding Hotel. The first man to greet them was Augustus B. Wolvin, whom everyone called Gus.

Where awkwardness seemed likely, Coulby and Wolvin got along well as lifelong friends. Never mind that Coulby had replaced Wolvin the year before as the Pittsburgh Steamship president, seizing control of the 112-vessel fleet whose inventory outnumbered that of the U.S. Navy.

Wolvin's short tenure at the helm was punctuated by labor tension, rising operating costs, and plenty of wrecked and stranded boats—none of which much affected his stature among Duluth's elite.

In fact, Wolvin was doing just fine. He had financial stakes in several shipping interests. He'd moved the Duluth office of the Pittsburgh Steamship Company into the seventh floor of a handsome new office tower on First Street named, fittingly enough, the Wolvin Building.

In the summer of 1904, three months after relinquishing the reins of the Pittsburgh fleet to Coulby, Wolvin was beaming on an April Saturday at the shipyard on the Black River near Lorain, Ohio. He smashed a bottle of champagne on the yellow nose of a 5,000-deadweight-ton, 560-foot, state-of-the-art steamship. With revolutionary hatches and sloping cargo holds, the boat was nicknamed the Yellow Kid because of its mustard hue from waterline down. It was the new king of the Great Lakes.

"I christen thee the *Augustus B. Wolvin*," Gus Wolvin proclaimed to a cheering throng.

A season later, Wolvin's jaw went slack as he peered out the seventh-floor window. He watched the *Mataafa* rise up and nosedive off the lake bottom, veering off the north pier head.

Wolvin immediately took charge, or tried to. He gathered together fifty men, sending employees to fetch the lifesavers from their boathouse station at the canal. They found no one and learned about the fatal twist of fate. The lifesavers had scurried two miles down the beach to rescue a ship that didn't need much rescuing—the beached *R. W. England*.

In the plush, velvety hotel suite at the Spaulding, flames crackled in the fireplace and light danced off thick drapes. Wolvin explained all this to the sour-faced Coulby. H. W. Brown, the local Pittsburgh office manager, fought off exhaustion and augmented Wolvin's detailed report.

A dozen Tin Stackers of the Pittsburgh fleet had been crippled by the blow. A dozen of their sailors were dead. When Thanksgiving dawned that Thursday, Wolvin and Coulby left the Spaulding Hotel for a brisk walk to the Wolvin Building. They clattered up the elevator and wouldn't be seen all day by Mary McFadden and other reporters who were stalking their comings and goings.

Ship captains were shuttled into the office, including Dick Humble off the *Mataafa*, Frank Rice off the *Crescent City*, A. J. Talbot off the *Edenborn*, and Dell Wright off the *Lafayette*, which had crashed between its barge and Encampment Island six miles north of Two Harbors.

Coulby listened to the damage reports, puffed a cigar, and started forging priorities. The *Crescent City* would have to be pulled off the rocks first, lest another storm slice the cracked hull and sink it in deep water. That would jack up the salvage costs dramatically.

Coulby, Wolvin, and others decided the *Mataafa* could wait until spring. All the damage was done. Two large cracks had fractured its hull. There it would sit all winter, seven hundred feet off shore, just off the north pier, reminding the people of Duluth every day about the horrors they'd witnessed.

Coulby sent Smith up the shore on the steamer *Manola* to Two Harbors. He then rode the tug *Edna G.* up to see the *Edenborn* propped safely on boulders near where its barge, the *Madeira*, had sunk at Gold Rock just north of Split Rock. When Smith returned on the tug to Duluth, he told Coulby and the assorted captains, mates, and marine surveyors a trivial bit of news that prompted bursts of disgust:

When the *Crescent City* crew hustled off to seek shelter at the Lakewood Pumping Station, a thieving gang of beachcombers had ransacked the stranded steamship. They took money, jewelry, glasses, barometers, life preservers, even the megaphone. They'd left drawers yanked askew in the rooms of the captain, mate, and wheelman.

What really galled Coulby and the others on the seventh floor was this: The thieves had even stolen turkeys out of the icebox, robbing the *Crescent City* crewmates of their Thanksgiving supper.

Darkness set in on Duluth as many celebrated a bittersweet Thanksgiving, falling so soon after the storm's drama had played out

The Wolvin Building, named after Gus Wolvin, served as the headquarters
for the hard-hit Pittsburgh Steamship Company. President Harry Coulby
called all the captains in after the storm for individual meetings with him
and Wolvin. *Minnesota Historical Society*

up and down Lake Superior's North Shore. Coulby strode from the
Wolvin Building back to the Spaulding Hotel, wrapped in an overcoat and surrounded by Smith, Duluth marine surveyor Joe Kidd,
and a half dozen shipmasters and mates.

In a crowded hotel lobby, Harry Coulby read a statement he had
crafted that afternoon. Mary McFadden and other newspaper people
were provided copies:

While I have been in Duluth I have heard there was some criticism on the street of the tardiness of the lifesaving crew in rendering assistance to the *Mataafa*. I do not think the criticism is warranted, from the fact that they had no knowledge that the *Mataafa* would need their services, and, as the steamer *England* was in distress, it was, of course, their first duty to go to her.

Around Duluth, the chief lifesaver, Murdoch McLennan, was receiving most of the blame and barbs. In two sentences, Coulby acknowledged the talk and debunked it. He then played the Gus Wolvin card, knowing his rich predecessor remained popular and influential in Duluth:

"Captain A. B. Wolvin, who is still connected with the Steel Corporation, was standing in his window when he saw the *Mataafa* entering the piers and saw the first sign of trouble, and he was on the ground immediately and did everything that man could possibly do to promptly aid the *Mataafa*."

If Wolvin was still connected to U.S. Steel, Coulby certainly wasn't going to question his effort. Coulby told the newspaper reporters how Wolvin gathered one hundred men, sending some on a tug to fetch the lifesaving apparatus. Coulby's praise for Gus Wolvin was thick:

"Captain Wolvin is, of course, recognized, by reason of his long and varied experience in like matters, to be eminently competent to look after matters of this kind, and rendered all the assistance that was possible, and nobody deplores it more than I do that we were unable to save the entire crew."

Coulby chose his words with great care. He picked "deplore" over a verb such as "regret" and opted for "unable to save" to describe frozen and drowned employees. Now it was time to confront the more egregious theme of the sidewalk second-guessing—with his chest puffed out:

"I also understand there have been rumors that the boats of this company are expected to leave port immediately after they are loaded, regardless of the weather conditions. I am quite unable to understand how such a rumor as this should get abroad for the reason that it is in direct contradiction to the positive orders the masters of our steamers have had repeatedly."

Coulby's English temper flared:

"The company spares no expense to keep its ships absolutely seaworthy and our captains have positive orders that no one of the company will be permitted to give them any orders as to when they shall leave port or seek shelter."

Captain Dick Humble was, no doubt, listening in the Spaulding Hotel when Coulby delivered the U.S. Steel company line. Odds are Coulby warned his master in advance that the corporate finger would point directly at Humble, even if he didn't single him out by name.

They were the masters, after all.

"They are on the ground and are expected to keep themselves posted on the weather conditions and to use their own judgment not only as to when they should leave port but in all matters concerning the navigation of their ships."

Coulby then rattled off the Steel Trust's roster of storm victims, both steel-hulled and human:

> *Edenborn* ashore on Split Rock. The third assistant engineer (James Johnson) unfortunately fell in the hold of the vessel and was killed.
>
> The steel barge *Madeira* dashed herself to pieces on the rocks. . . . The mate (James Morrow), when the ship struck the rocks, went up into the mizzen rigging and was not seen afterward.
>
> The steamer *Lafayette* went ashore on or near Encampment Island and is a total loss.

Coulby went on to talk about the varied fates of the barge *Manila*, the *Crescent City*, the *Coralia*, the *Maia*, and, of course, the *Mataafa*. He first addressed the chances of salvaging each vessel, then reported the dozen deaths. The only victim mentioned by name was Gilchrist, the *Mataafa*'s oiler who had washed away and not been found. His father was in Duluth, possibly in the room, glaring at the corporate boss and prompting his son's name to be called.

When he was done, Coulby evaded most of the questions about the breakwater scheme and the lifesavers' delay. He continued to steadfastly point the finger of blame at the weather and Captain Humble's decision to sail into it.

"I have no criticism to make of the harbor, or the lifesaving crew, or anything except the weather, which cannot be helped," Coulby said.

Whether it was a calculated strategy to divert culpability or what he truly believed, Coulby didn't waiver. He blamed the weather and the captain for all that had happened.

Despite all Coulby's claims, newspaperwoman Mary McFadden, weatherman Herbert Richardson, and the guys at Lanigan's pub all wondered, in the back of their minds, just how much blame Coulby could pass off to others' shoulders. He'd taken over the Pittsburgh Steamship Company one season before. He'd fought the unions and flexed control, from Cleveland, over every deckhand hiring and harbor docking. He represented the Great Lakes sailing arm of U.S. Steel, the nation's first megamerger conglomerate.

And McFadden remembered a three-week-old quote in her newspaper. It was attributed to Allyn Harvey, one of Coulby's subordinates, and he hinted at the bust-the-bottom-line backdrop Coulby carefully avoided in his prepared remarks.

"We shall be very pleased if November turns out to be milder than usual," Harvey told the newspaper on November 7, 1905. "The month will show up strong in the ore shipping column for the season if conditions are favorable. The impression prevails that we shall have a late season, and that would be welcomed by shipping interests."

XI

"The unjust criticism of the general public has stung the noble captain to the quick."

~ *The Labor World*
December 2, 2005

Mary McFadden had heard so much whispering and cussing directed toward Captain Murdoch McLennan's lifesaving crew, she knew she must seek him out. Never mind that it was Thanksgiving morning. The plucky newspaperwoman trudged down to the beach at Minnesota Point and found the U.S. Lifeboat House. The simple, two-story timber structure was shrouded with shingles and supported on railroad ties. A simple wooden bridge, sporting some benches, connected the boathouse and the shore. A tall flagpole, stripped from a pine tree, was planted nearby.

McFadden waited until she saw the captain land his surf boat on the beach. Splash and spray frosted his dark mustache. He told

Mary McFadden, photographed here in 1899, was Duluth's first newspaperwomen. *Photo by Charles A. Zimmerman, Minnesota Historical Society*

her he had been assisting the tugs as they tried to dredge and draw the steamer *England* off the shore and into deeper water.

McFadden followed the captain into the boathouse and up the ladder, where they sat by a small woodstove in the crew quarters. McLennan had previously declined McFadden's interview request, but now she followed him into the loft. As captain, McLennan had a small room with a desk, a bed, and a pair of casement windows— eight panes on top and a dozen on the bottom half.

"You know, captain, that many have said your crew was negligent in the work of saving the crew on the *Mataafa*? Will you tell me your view of the situation?"

She had her pen ready, but only silence followed. McLennan was visibly affected. It surprised Mary. She had worked hard to corner him for this interview. Now she realized there were tears in his chestnut eyes.

McFadden would write in the next day's *Duluth News Tribune*:

> There seemed to be tears in his heart at the thought that he had striven hard and faithfully and had through failure to save all met with criticism and lack of confidence from those who watched his labors.
>
> The great bulk of the man was stamped with utter weariness. This he bore manfully, but the discredit cast upon his courage and his ability and that of his crew cut him like a whip.

McFadden waited for McLennan to speak. She made it clear she wasn't leaving until she had his words, his response, which she would publish Friday for all the people who had tried to help. And for those who merely gawked and crowded tightly around McLennan's crew. The second-guessers, Mary McFadden knew, would gobble up every word.

Finally, the large Scottish captain wiped his mustache with the back of his hand, exhaled, and spoke in the halting voice of a crying man:

"A man may do his duty to the uttermost and still be the victim of criticism. I have known of this censure which has been passed upon the crew, generally, and particularly upon myself and it has cut."

He poured himself some coffee and sipped it.

"It is a bitter thing to work when the muscles ache, when the brain in fagged and when a man's whole being cries out for rest; to fail in a measure and then have it said that one should have succeeded; I do not want to say anything. This matter will likely be investigated by the department, and I will report to them. But I feel sick about it and do not want to talk."

Mary McFadden suppressed a smile. She knew she had primed the pump but kept pumping with both hands. "But there are thousands of people who, rightly or wrongly, blame you and your men for the loss of nine human lives. Can you afford to remain silent either in justice to the people, the steamship company, or yourself and your men?"

McFadden's own pump, too, had been primed. She continued to pepper the exhausted lifesaver with questions she'd heard repeated across Duluth. "It has been said that you waited at the wrecked *England* after those men were safe and while precious hours of light, during which the best chances of saving the men on the *Mataafa*, were flying by. Why did you not come sooner?"

Mary McFadden redipped her quill in an ink well and waited until Murdoch McLennan exploded with words, defending his men and pointing the finger of blame back at the crowds that had been belittling him.

> We came as soon as we could. As soon as we knew of the condition of the *Mataafa* we started out at once and hastened desperately to the scene. That we were too late was no fault of ours, nor of anyone's that I can think of.
>
> Word was brought to me as I worked getting off the ten men on the *England* whose plight I do not and never did think dangerous after I arrived on the scene. But as long as we knew of no other wreck it was our bounden duty to remain by the *England*.

The newspaperwoman's claim, that they had somehow dilly-dallied, irked McLennan.

When we were told of the plight of the *Mataafa*, we started at once with the whole crew and the beach cart. We did not even wait to cast off our line from the *England*.

It was then three o'clock, and the men who had been awake and alert all night, who had hauled the cart two and half miles through soft sand, piled snowdrifts, and water could not make the distance of more than three miles, not including the ferry and detours through the woods made necessary by the condition of the beach, in any less time than one and a half hours, which was the time we took.

We arrived at the beach in front of the *Mataafa* at about 4:30, but it was five o'clock when the first shot was fired. We fired again and missed a second time. That used up all our prepared lines and we had to get another line in shape. We used that, but as you saw, though it landed on the boat, it was entangled and finally cut by the wreckage and the rocks.

McLennan hesitated before directly responding to criticism of the throngs with some barbs of his own. He knew defending his men was the noble thing to do, but his anger and exhaustion were such that he could no longer refrain from unleashing his own volley.

We were badly hampered by the encroachments of a crowd which, while it had time for criticism and senseless suggestions, had none for the thought that its crowding in eagerness to see was retarding our efforts to accomplish what I cannot but think was our common end.

We did not stop work until eleven o'clock, and then at the request of Mr. Waterson, an official of the company owning the boat, who declared that he had heard Captain Humble of the *Mataafa* shout through a megaphone that the men were safe and all forward. He said also, he thought they would not come ashore, even though a line was passed to them, as that would be more dangerous than to remain on board. A line was fast to the ship at that time.

The accusations of laziness hurt McLennan more than any other.

"I did not sleep that night. I did not even sit down and the men did little better. We were doing killing work under conditions, which from being bad at the start grew steadily worse, by reason of the increasing cold."

McFadden let him catch his breath before tossing him another question: "It has been repeatedly said that you could have launched your surf boat and that in that way the men might have been taken off. Do you believe that would have been possible, and, if so, why was it not done?"

McLennan made a sound like a horse, popping air from the lips below the mustache.

It was utterly, hopelessly impossible. We never could have got the boat out from the beach before the *Mataafa*. It would have been smashed upon the rocks or by the debris. The boats are light, necessarily, and are easily broken. Launching from the beach was impossible.

It was equally impossible to have a boat towed out into the lake, as no tug would venture out in that sea. We could not have won to the ship if we had launched on the other side of the canal, and if we had launched on the harbor side we never could have got out.

This is terrible. There is no man in Duluth who feels the loss of those men more than I do, but I was powerless when the shot lines failed, and knew it.

Mary McFadden asked one more question, about the lack of a search light, which McLennan agreed might have helped. He was clearly tired, and she knew she had more than enough for tomorrow's *Tribune*.

In the end, several odd bedfellows would come to Murdoch McLennan's defense. Harry Coulby, president of the Pittsburgh Steamship Company, had insisted at his press gathering that all the criticism aimed at the lifesaving captain was unwarranted. From the other end of the spectrum, the workers' voice in Duluth, *The Labor World*, insisted that a lack of resources limited the crew to aid only one vessel at a time:

Whatever word of criticism may have been uttered in regard to the work of Capt. McLennan and his noble lifesavers, *The Labor World* is convinced that owing to the insufficiency of equipment, they were greatly handicapped. It is impossible for us to think that a man of Capt. McLennan's kindly nature would fail to use every possible effort to rescue suffering humanity in whatever position they were placed.

Even the investigator from the U.S. Life-Saving Service concluded that the timing of the *England*'s beaching more than two miles away—not McLennan's leadership—doomed the *Mataafa*.

"If they had not gone to the assistance of the steamer *R. W. England*, they would doubtless have been able to save some of if not all of those on the after part of the vessel. As the situation stood," the officer's report stated, "the loss of life that occurred was inevitable, and is in no way chargeable to the station crew. They seem to have done all that lay in their power."

Whether any of that support from the corporation, the government, and the unions could actually heal all the harpoon gashes from the shore critics would be hard to gauge. But when McLennan died twenty-five years later, the newspaper would devote only four sentences to his passing—tucked in a small column of four Duluth death notices:

Funeral services for Capt. M. A. McLennan, retired commander
of the United States coast guard station here, who died Monday

in his home, 1114 E. Mankato St., will be held Wednesday at the First Presbyterian Church. Burial will be in the Forest Hill cemetery. Surviving are his widow; one son Alex, and a daughter, Mrs. Runcie Martin, Duluth. Captain McLennan retired from active duty in 1924, after serving in the coast guard for 37 years.

XII

"There is no life so smooth and well regulated but that may be assailed by an unexpected crisis just as those ships on the stormy billows of the lake and many a life is wrecked because the anchor of faith in the Divine Pilot failed to bear the stress of wind and wave."

~The Reverend H. W. Smith, pastor of the
Plymouth Congregational Church
December 3, 1905

Duluth's taverns, churches, and municipal court all saw business boom in the days following the storm. Sympathy for the hundred stranded sailors roaming the city ran as freely as the ale from the kegs at Lanigan's. When one of the weary seamen wandered into a saloon, if the bartender hadn't already set him up with a free round, a bystander would surely pick up the tab and offer a toast to the sailor's survival. Before long, sailors were stumbling between bars in Duluth and Superior, unable to recall their own names. Or, they hoped, the details of the deadly storm they'd just endured.

Charlie Byrne was among the drunken sailors. A *Mataafa* fireman from Buffalo, Byrne was the last of the three men to successfully dash between giant waves to get from the stern to the forepeak. By Saturday afternoon, Charlie was decked out in a new suit of clothes with a month's pay in his pocket. He stood, or tried to, before Superior Police Chief William McKinnon.

"Yes, I have weathered many a storm," he told the chief, slurring his words. "But I will have to admit that your Superior booze has got the best of me this time."

McKinnon tried to pump some stories out of him, but Charlie shook his head.

"I am not in shape to tell you all about the wreck until I have slept some of this off and then, if you are around, I will tell you all about it."

The chief folded his arms and considered sending Byrne down the hallway to court on the charge of public intoxication. So the fireman spoke up to defend himself.

"You see, between the two storms I am very much under the weather, but I know you won't be too harsh with me. I simply had to do something to drive away the thoughts of that awful catastrophe which has been on my mind ever since it took place."

He pulled out his Marine Fireman Union card and other documents to prove he was indeed part of the *Mataafa* crew. The chief sat silently for a moment and then smiled and said in a booming voice for all gathered to hear:

"Although you have violated one of our city ordinances, you certainly have my sympathy."

McKinnon ordered one of his officers to lead Charlie Byrne to a cot. And once he sobered up, Byrne was released. He left Superior and landed in a Duluth tavern. By Monday morning, he was trying to stand in front of Duluth Municipal Judge Frank Cutting. Coulby's underlings at the office had sent word to the judge that Byrne would be placed on the next downbound boat once he showed up at the Wolvin Building.

"Suspended sentence," Judge Cutting announced.

The gushing sympathy of the cops and courts soon faded. Take the case of Walter Crane, a British deckhand with a flowery tongue. He had been one of the first of the drenched and shivering crewmembers of the *R. W. England* to be shuttled ashore by the lifesavers' breeches buoy.

Crane headed straight from the beach to the bar, where his exhausted state and empty stomach made him easy prey to the alcohol's ill effects. A policeman found him wandering the streets on that first Wednesday night. If the cop hadn't stumbled upon the stumbling Crane, the sailor likely would have passed out and frozen to death.

Instead, he fought to maintain his balance before Municipal Judge William Windom.

"I was so glad to be alive after the storm," he told the judge. "And I was so cold and exhausted and wet to the skin, that I had to warm up a little, and I guess I took too many before I knew it."

In his thick English accent, Walter Crane assured the judge he "meant no harm, and if you will let me go, I will go to work. I am industrious, and will not loiter about this city."

The judge was convinced and magnanimous. He put himself in the wet sailor's boots and shrugged inside his robe.

"Probably a majority of men would have committed the same offense under similar circumstances," Windom ruled. "I am satisfied that many men would have done exactly the same as you, and I shall suspend the sentence."

Crane, hat in his hand, bowed in appreciation and thanked the judge. The newspaper's court reporter wrote that "the court officers were nearly weeping on his neck when he left."

Crane promptly bumped into a crewmate named Martin Anderson from the *England* and, naturally, they ducked into a bar within blocks of the courthouse. When Crane returned to court the next day to face a charge of public drunkenness, the judge's mood had soured.

"Don't you think you are working this stranded sailor story a little too strong?" Judge Windom asked.

The newspaperman in court insisted Crane's "story was just as good as it was yesterday, but the effect had warn off somewhat."

Windom suspended Anderson's sentence and fined Crane ten dollars, which would be waived if he boarded a boat or a train and left Duluth within twelve hours.

"If we don't check up on this, every prisoner that comes in here for the next week will be homeless sailors stranded by the storm," Judge Windom warned. "This movement promises to become too popular. I don't want to see all our clients here turn sailors."

Still, the sympathy ran high. As one unnamed court officer told the *Duluth Evening Tribune* that Saturday:

> You can't blame them much for getting drunk. Everybody is offering them free drinks, and after such an experience as they went through, most of them are ready to take a drink. If they go into a saloon the bartender promptly sets up the drinks, or if he fails to do it, some of the bystanders will propose a drink to celebrate their escape from a watery grave.
>
> Everybody knows who they are and wants to buy them a drink or a cigar, and those who are at all inclined to drink

have every opportunity to get full. When you consider that there are more than one hundred wrecked sailors in town, and that all have come through an experience that they will never forget, it is a wonder we have not had more of them in here.

A sailor always wants to celebrate when he strikes shore, anyway, and it would be a queer sailor who wouldn't feel like celebrating after such an experience as that.

Likewise, it would be a queer sailor who would skip church that Sunday morning. Every sermon, it seemed, tried to make sense of the chaos, the rescues, and the deaths.

At the First Norwegian-Danish church, the Reverend H. K. Madsen delivered a morning memorial service entitled "A Drifting Ship." At Grace Methodist, the Reverend Joseph Robinson spent the morning discussing "A Call for Help," while his evening service explored "Drifting Off the Track of the Home Ships."

Inside the large, dark red-purple stones of his Richardson Romanesque church on the incline of East Second Street, the Reverend T. H. Cleland at First Presbyterian discussed "The Inward Truth" in the morning and "The Great Lakes Tragedy" after nightfall. And two blocks over, the brick Pilgrim Congregational Church stood on a frosty, expansive lawn with its squared-off central tower and adjoining vaulted roofed chapel. The Reverend Alexander Milne lectured on a theme that weaved its way through all the services: "The Sacredness of Human Life."

Over on Duluth's East End, the First Methodist Church steeple pointed high atop the Old World Tudor architecture. People packed the pews. The women wore billowy black Victorian dresses and massive decorative hats, the men long coats and fine hats of their own. Throughout the storm, the Reverend Merton Rice had been a regular fixture in the crowds around the bonfires. He had watched the *Mataafa* survivors snake down the rope to the lifeboat an hour before he saw five frozen bodies chipped off the afterdeck.

Merton Rice had spent all week writing and rewriting his sermon, "The Wreck of the *Mataafa*." He wasn't a bit surprised when he stepped up in his pulpit and saw every pew filled for the evening service. His sermon recounted the spectacle in great detail but first pointed to the Scriptures, Acts 27:41, and John's voyage and shipwreck en route to Rome:

"And when we were fallen into a place where two seas met, they run the ship aground. And the forepart indeed, sticking fast, remained unmoveable: but the hinder part was broken with the violence of the waves."

Then Merton Rice shared his firsthand account, gleaned from the throng that lined the beach:

The steel sheathed *Ellwood* staggered through the canal, where she might sink down to rest in a protected place. We cheered our throats sore at her crew of happy men as they got in.

Through the spray the *England*'s black hull showed large where she had run up on the sands, and we hoped her men were safe. And the *Pope* came running in a mottled course, back and forth, swung by wave and current and wind, but she ran past us, scarred by the teeth of the angry storm that had bitten off great portions of the woodwork.

And we cheered again and again under the common impulse of mere men saved from the storm. And away on the tossing horizon another black signal was hoisted of the coming of another to feel safety in the harbor. The speculations were rife when we saw the great steamer laboring hard at a towing barge. All knew that together they could not enter.

Captain Humble had known the same thing, which is why he released the rope linking the *Mataafa* and its consort, the *Nasmyth*. Reverend Rice looked out at his parishioners, who typically were yawning, whispering, or dozing. Tonight, they gave him their full attention. And he was on a roll.

When the barge was dropped outside, our wonder was doubled at the different fates to be risked here. And our prayers were lifted for the splendid ship that, loaded down in the awful sea, once more set her prow for the entrance home.

She shuddered as the storm swept the cushion of waters from under her and let her strike heavily on the bottom. The crash was heard, the quivering creature of steel had recoiled, and the constantly imperiled men were running across the decks, and the great ship was pounding like a huge hammer in the hands of the seas against the adamant anvil of the pier to make the thousands groan and cry at every stroke.

The reverend had been equally breathless when he joined the crowds on the shore. Five days later, his memories were nearly as haunting as the sight of the actual collision of the *Mataafa* and the pier.

My God! I shall never forget the snap of the rigging when she struck. I shall never lose from my eye the desperation of those clinging men as the great *Mataafa* swung slowly about and pushed in on the rocks ashore. The hissing groan of the steam robbed whistle, the clustering men, their cry for help. The hungry, eager crowd, close enough to talk to them and yet as empty of ability to do as though they had been a thousand miles away. The scouring consciousness of the little distance they were away was enough to drive us mad, and we stamped the washed shore and condemned our weakness.

Reverend Rice reminded his parishioners what they all had learned too plainly five days earlier.

O man, what a frail creature you are! How helpless after all you are! Where men's lives, or great interests are in the balance, nothing is more exciting than to watch the uncertain issue, or more gratifying than to see life saved, the dead alive, the lost found.

Nine men have died before our very eyes, they looking hungrily at us, we, in safety, helplessly gazing at their struggles to live. It sobered our judgments and put the cap of solemn thoughts on every soul in our city.

Sometimes we would think the one thought of the world was how to evolve more of its treasures; and at times some studious pessimistic soul rises to tell us that we care not for the men who pay the price. Well, maybe at the time we do act as though this judgment were just, but I declare it to be false.

It was all the comfort I could extract from the awful scene. It was the great unconscious captain of the thoughts and actions of the horrified thousands there. Above all us down deeper than all, the worth of the men who toil here— these men we love above all else we have. Why none could ever describe the feeling that had our hearts; that queer cry that came from all men's souls as they witnessed the hero who three times hurled over the deck pulled himself up as by superhuman power where he could run back to the sure death awaiting him.

He was referring to Thomas Woodgate, the fireman from Toronto, whose body was just then arriving home. His father the fruit merchant would be waiting. He'd written the letter, tucked in his son's pocket, with a final salutation: "I now say bye bye as I hope soon to see you."

Reverend Rice, underneath the towering steeple, told his flock:

Men think more of each other than they know they do. It may take the storm to teach us; but we are helpless to put it in practice there save as we shiveringly build bonfires and wait for the sea to run down a little.

Make your fellow men know by your actions in the days when you can reach them and help them, you appreciate their real worth. It will solve every problem of living. Listen! No more eloquent sermon was ever hurled into the souls of Duluth than the fact that there is no safe place until you are safely through the gates into the eternal city.

Inside. It is dreadful to perish in sight of deliverance and home. It is the story of that soul almost persuaded to become a Christian. Get within the gates, my friends.

Merton Rice's church, on the East End of Duluth, sat across town from Plymouth Congregational Church, on the West End. The messages of the sermon, like the rapt attention of those in the pews, mirrored each other.

The Reverend H. W. Johnson at Plymouth Congregational titled his talk "On the Rocks."

"Storms of life," he said, with his hands on the pulpit and his voice clear and loud enough to be heard perfectly in the back of the church, "are best weathered by meeting them squarely in the face."

> The harrowing experiences of the last week have been perhaps the worst that this city or any of the lake ports have ever witnessed. And next to the deep pity with which we regard the tragic death of so many men in the discharge of their duties our feelings are stirred by the admiration which we are compelled to bear for the deeds of the heroism performed in the saving of lives and vessels by those who weathered the gale.

> What makes the disaster more deplorable is the fact that so many of the men lost their lives within sight of thousands powerless to render assistance and one might say on the threshold of the harbor where they expected rest and shelter.

Blame, a sport that had consumed Duluth since the storm subsided, found its way into Johnson's sermon.

"Apparently all that human effort could do was done to prevent the loss of life, and through lack of proper or sufficient appliances the life service crew was not able to do all that the men might have done; there is no use in attaching blame to the men themselves."

There were larger issues than doling out fault and the reverend, as he was wont to do, hoped to raise the discussion.

"The great point for us to consider is that the marines perished on the verge of salvation and what a lesson this teaches us in the voyage of life where so many go down to destruction with salvation at their doors."

The drunken sailors in the street and the courts, sobered up for the sermon, looked down when the preacher turned to non-Christian influences:

Even as it was not sufficient for those mariners to be near the harbor, so it is not enough for a soul to be within the shadow of the church and daily within the shore of Christian influences.

The only safety lies in complete measures of salvation and right inside the harbor of God's kingdom. There is no life so smooth and well regulated but that may be assailed by an unexpected crisis, just as those ships on the stormy billows of the lake and many a life is wrecked because the anchor of faith in the Divine Pilot failed to bear the stress of wind and wave.

The best of human efforts sometimes proves unavailing, and human judgment is liable to error just as no human power could have foreseen the awful storm and the destruction that was to follow.

And the wise voyager on life's highway must keep his eye fixed on the higher counsels of Almighty God.

But once caught in the storm, the wise lesson which we must deduce from these boats is to meet the peril in the face and with determination and endurance, ride out the blast.

Oh, that all of us in the day of trial and temptation might remember the example taught by the brave mariner and never turn our backs to the billows until the storm has ceased and we can ride into the harbor on the wings of peace.

Mataafa Crew Roster

Saved:

Richard F. Humble, Master, Conneaut, Ohio

Walter F. Brown, First Mate, Detroit, Michigan

Herbert W. Emigh, Second Mate, Lexington, Michigan

George McClure, Wheelsman, Amadore, Michigan

James Hatch, Wheelsman, Winnipeg, Ontario

Grantley West, Watchman, Own Sound, Ontario

Ernest Dietz, Watchman, Winnipeg, Ontario

Fred Saunders, Porter, Amherstburg, Ontario

James Suttle, Deckhand, Winnipeg, Ontario

Harry Larson, Deckhand, Superior, Wisconsin

Leon Yake, Deckhand, Lexington, Michigan

Lewis Yates, Deckhand, Lexington, Michigan

Axel Carlson, Fireman, Chicago, Illinois

Edward Coulter, Fireman, address unknown

Charles Byrne, Fireman, Buffalo, New York

Ice coats the *Mataafa's* stern following the epic storm. *Photo by Hugh McKenzie, Lake Superior Maritime Collections, UW–Superior*

Lost:

William Most, Chief Engineer, Chicago, Illinois

C. A. Farenger, Second Engineer, Cleveland, Ohio

James Early, Third Engineer, Buffalo, New York

Carl Carlson, Oiler, Chicago, Illinois

William Gilchrist, Oiler, Wiarton, Ontario

Henry Wright, Steward, Cleveland

Walter Bush, Cook, Amherstburg, Ontario

Thomas McCloud, Deckhand, Brandenburg, Kentucky

PART 4

The Scow, the Umbria, and the Owen

I

"Why, I have sailed this lake for fifteen years and never dreamed that the wind could play such havoc. It was awful and no language of mine can make you understand the relentless force, the power of that storm."

~ _Lafayette_ first mate F. D. Seeley
November 30, 1905

"It was so dark, and the storm so furious, it was impossible to face it."

~ Scow skipper Charles Johnson of Duluth
December 1, 1905

The phone clanged and jangled in the downtown office of Louis Martin. The call came from Ole Miller's brick flat on 28th Avenue West and Third Street. A feathery female voice, that of a sailor's niece, asked if there was news about the scow.

Yes, she was told. Captain Charlie Johnson and William Hicks, the clerk from the lumber camp, had returned to Duluth from eighty miles up the North Shore by Two Islands.

"Is Ole Miller back?"

Louis Martin exhaled and closed his eyes. He had leased his flat-bottomed scow, *George Herbert*, to the M. H. Coolidge Lumber Company. It was loaded with provisions—smoked meats, coffee, whiskey, and lard—for the lumber camp up the shore. The tugboat *F. W. Gillett* towed the scow, its supplies, and a five-man crew: Captain Johnson, lumber clerk Hicks, Ole Miller, George Olson, and Ole Nelson. They all hailed from Duluth. They had been among the first ones slapped by the gale, which hit the North Shore that Monday afternoon, some four hours before it bore down on Duluth.

Three nights later, on Thanksgiving, when Charlie Johnson walked, shivering, through the door of his house at 624 Second Avenue West, his wife, Marie, looked picket-fence white. She sobbed with convulsions, looking at Charlie as if he were a ghost. The fear that had squeezed her since the storm struck was now finally loosening. She clamped Charlie into a smothering embrace.

They stoked the fireplace and snuggled under heavy woolen blankets, a warm whiskey in Charlie Johnson's raw hand. He walked her backward through the nightmarish days since he'd seen her last, since his scow had splintered on the rocks eighty miles up the North Shore at Two Islands.

He and Bill Hicks, the lumber camp's agent, had caught a ride back to Duluth on the tug *Crosby*. They'd trudged six miles down the North Shore to Thomasville, a tiny fisherman's village. That's where they found the crewmates of the bulk freighter *George Spencer* and its barge, *Amboy*, which were carrying coal from Buffalo for Duluth's Northwestern Fuel Company. Both boats had wrecked and tangled on the rocks nearby.

All twenty-two men on the two boats were saved, Johnson learned, thanks to the bravery of the fishermen of Thomasville and some lumbermen from a nearby camp. As they tossed back toward Duluth on the tug, Johnson listened to the captain of the *Spencer*, Frank Conlin, share his ship's ordeal.

His crew had suffered horribly through the frozen night. About noon Tuesday, the boat was wrecked on the rocks, some two hundred yards offshore. The crew fastened a rope to a plank and tossed it in, hoping it would float to shore.

The *Spencer*'s crew could make out the faint outline of fishermen on the beach. With ropes tied around their chests, a few waded breast-deep into the freezing, slapping surf. One of them grabbed the plank as he lost his feet, only to be hauled back to shore by his mates.

Conlin told the crowd gathered around him on the tug how, with one line fastened to a tree and another line connected to the boat, a chair had been fastened to the lower line and all fifteen in his crew and all nine aboard the barge *Amboy* had been rescued. The barge's 1,500 tons of coal were gone. The boat's bottom had been crashed in. Conlin figured his coal could be lightered out, but his boat was a total wreck.

"What about your ordeal?" Mrs. Johnson had patiently waited for her husband to share his nightmare. He stared ahead, sipped his whiskey, and spoke softly. About one o'clock Monday afternoon, it had started to blow hard. By three o'clock, they reached Two Islands, and it was blowing a gale. In addition to Charlie Johnson and Hicks, three others were on the scow—Ole Miller, Ole Nelson, and George Olson.

Johnson told his wife how they'd gotten behind the islands. The lee side offered protection from the wind in the summer months. But not this time of year. His tug, *F. W. Gillett*, dropped its anchor, and so did Johnson. The towline connecting the two held fast.

That night, the men rotated two-man teams, five-minute shifts each, checking the towline to make sure it held. But the night was so dark and stormy, they couldn't face the icy, pelting lake. So they stood, backs to the storm, hands on the towline.

At about one o'clock Tuesday morning, the line snapped. Johnson was aft.

Johnson paused and looked into his wife's eyes, then continued. Olson and Nelson were up front, on watch. Within five minutes, the scow struck shore, zipping like lightning once the towline parted. Three times the scow smashed into the rocks, a little higher up the shore each time.

On the third collision, Hicks took a running jump and leaped off the back of the scow and onto a rock that was sticking up on the shore. Johnson followed his lead. When he landed, he scrambled as fast as he could to a higher outcrop. But a wave grabbed him, swept him off the rocks, and tossed him up a little higher on the rocky shore. He and Hicks climbed to the bluff top, out of the icy water's reach.

Ole Miller, George Olson, and Ole Nelson had shouted goodbye when Johnson and Hicks jumped. The three men were dashing up and down on the deck, too frightened to leap. Their farewell yells were the last Johnson or Hicks would hear from them.

The two survivors found a settler's cabin, where a Mrs. Kenny and her son provided warm blankets, steaming coffee, and soup. The sailors slept by her fire.

The next day, Johnson and Hicks hunted up and down the shore, looking for the other three men. But all they found was kindling wood that had formerly been their scow. About two hundred feet inland from the shoreline, Charlie found a piece of towline and an anchor.

After hours of scouring the beach searching for bodies, they gave up and walked six miles south to Thomasville, where the *Spencer* and *Amboy* were wrecked and where the tug *Crosby* eventually came to give all the stranded men a ride back to Duluth.

If only Miller, Olson, and Nelson had jumped, too, Charlie told his wife, they might have survived. Staying on the scow was fatal. It broke up so quickly. Charlie's wife hugged him. Across town, Hicks and his family exhaled with relief, as well.

But there was no joy in the household at Second Avenue West and Sixth Street, where Ole Nelson's wife and six children now grieved. George Olson had been single and had buried his brother, Oscar, a few weeks earlier.

Family crowded into Ole Miller's brick flat at 28th Avenue West and Third Street. They surrounded his wife and four kids. A niece picked up the receiver of the Miller's telephone and the operator connected the line, Zenith 1636-Y, to Louis Martin's office in the harbor.

"Is Ole Miller back?" she asked.

As gently as he could, Louis Martin explained that Miller and two others were dashed on the rocks eighty miles up the North Shore. Their boat had splintered. They wouldn't be coming back.

II

"The sight of a heroic deed takes the fear from the most cowardly heart."

~ Andrew Cornaliusan, *Umbria*'s
second mate, from Cleveland
December 1, 1905

On Friday morning, the first dawn of December, Mary McFadden pinned her hair in a bun, whittled three pencil stubs into pointed tips, and slipped her notebook in her purse. She headed for the Boston coal docks at 37th Avenue West.

In all the reporting of the storm, McFadden had hardly slept. She had written countless column inches, detailing the names of the boats and their captains, their cargoes, their casualties, and their survivors. Yet she felt frustrated when she walked down the steps at 212 Ninth Avenue East, where she had rented a room the last two years.

The morning was cold but calm. The sky turned from turquoise to a deeper blue, as if washed by the three-day blow. McFadden walked as briskly as the morning air felt. It reddened her cheeks. Her goal was simple. She wanted to delve into the emotion beneath the storm. She wanted more from the stone-faced captains and mates who brushed aside her queries with a shrug and a "Merely doing our jobs, Ma'am."

The freighter *Umbria* came into Duluth with its pilot house steering destroyed. Sailors had to steer from the backup mechanism in the stern. *Minnesota Historical Society*

These sailors had endured trauma and drama unparalleled in Lake Superior lore. Everyone, even the older skippers, kept saying it had blown harder and longer than they had ever seen. Yet McFadden's notebook, to date, was filled with lengths, ports of origin, names of captains, but precious few feelings or human emotions. She wanted to describe how it felt inside the men when they clung to the rope rails on the swaying steamers, tossed liked seesaws in the waves.

Today, McFadden hoped, she would peel back the veneer of the leather-skinned sailors and pry a bit into their souls. She wanted to give some shape to the essential emotion a man faces when death roars so close. How does the communal sense of brotherhood, so bolted together on a steamship crew, manifest itself in times of peril and desperation?

She was so wrapped in thought, Mary McFadden gasped when she looked up and saw the *Umbria*, the massive crippled leviathan slumped in the waters of the Boston coal dock at 37th Avenue West. One of the largest boats on the lake at 420 feet, the *Umbria* had spilled out of the Cleveland shipyards two years earlier. And it was out of Cleveland where the ship started this voyage, hauling seven thousand tons of coal to Duluth for the H. A. Hawgood Company. Carrying ore from Minnesota over the lakes was cheaper than railroads, especially when the return trip could boost efficiency by hauling coal back up the thousand-mile watery highway. With winter about to set Duluth in its vice, coal was needed by the boatful.

The *Umbria* had sailed out of Sault Sainte Marie at nine o'clock Sunday night with a crew of twenty-two. The *Umbria* had no doubt gleamed as it spilled from the lock that night, its steel sides and the lake water reflecting the moonlight.

Mary McFadden loved the boat's name: *Umbria*. Unlike so many of the new bulk freights, which bore the names of cigar-chomping steel, shipping, and finance magnates, this boat took its name from the hilly central region of Italy—steeped in history, ancient and noble.

Yet now, as Mary McFadden gazed up at the big ship from her perch on the dock, her breath was snatched. Ice sheathed the big boat from stem to stern. Its pilot house had been stripped away, its roof collapsed by a giant billow. The shrouds were tangled. Windows shattered. Steel sides dented and battered. Cook smoke rose from all the chaos, men's voices filtering up with the smoke.

McFadden boarded the beat-up gangway and inquired about the whereabouts of Captain C. M. Seph's cabin. The men laughed deeply from their bellies. You'll need a diver's helmet to interview the captain in his cabin, they teased. The captain's quarters had been flooded in the darkness of Tuesday morning's combers.

Undaunted, Mary McFadden asked again for the captain, who her records showed came from Prairie View, north of Chicago. Most of the crew, like the *Umbria* itself, came from Cleveland. According to her records, a few of the men were from Milwaukee; Amherstburg, Ontario, near Detroit; even New York City. The watchmen were from Finland and Norway. Although Mary McFadden had become a familiar face on the docks over the last two years, most of the men on the bruised *Umbria* didn't know her from Eve.

Finally, a weathered sailor elbowed through the men and introduced himself to McFadden. Andrew Cornaliusan was the second mate from Cleveland. She asked him to spell his mouthful of a name slowly as she extracted her notebook and pencil from her purse. A gentleman among ruffians, Cornaliusan led McFadden to a nook in the cook's kitchen. He pulled up two folding chairs and agreed to answer any and all of her questions.

McFadden bit back her lip. This was the interview, she hoped, for which she had been longing. And when, before too long, tears rolled down the second mate's chapped cheeks, Mary felt at last she might have tapped a maple tree properly so the sweet syrup she had sought plucked into the pail.

Over the next half hour, Andrew Cornaliusan unselfishly pointed out the bravery of the wheelmen, the firemen, and Captain Seph. He shared his feelings of near-surrender and how they were overcome by shame, loyalty, and a communal spirit. Divinity, too, played a role.

"We sailed out of the Soo Locks at nine o'clock Sunday night," he began. The ship made twenty-four hours of solid westward progress across the vast Lake Superior. By nine o'clock Monday night, though, the clear cold calm had transformed into a gale. As the *Umbria* plowed between Eagle River and Outer Island of Michigan's Apostle group, the wind began to blow hard, and it didn't let up until Wednesday.

For four hours, Cornaliusan told McFadden as he stared into her eyes, the big boat held its own as the waves grew mountainous. By one o'clock Tuesday morning, Captain Seph ordered his wheelman to turn the bulk freighter into the walls of water. Better to face the fury head-on and dig through the troughs of the sea, he figured, than to roll broadside. But the largest of the waves promptly crashed over the bow, battering and shattering the *Umbria*'s pilot house up front. The roof came down, smashing the wheel, stripping the compasses, and taking away the green lights and the tanks. While panic would have been a natural reaction, Captain Seph resisted such urges. Instead, he calmly ordered his men to charge over the hurricane deck to the crippled ship's aft.

Cornaliusan wiped a tear away with the back of a thick hand and stared again with his coal-colored eyes into Mary McFadden's green irises.

"Under God and the coolness of the Captain," he told her, "we owe our lives to the bravery and endurance of the wheelmen, watchmen, and the forward crew."

Cornaliusan didn't blow his own whistle, although it became clear the captain had ordered Cornaliusan and the first mate, Joseph Richardson of Cleveland, to perform the most delicate of tasks in the most indelicate of circumstances imaginable. With icy waves slashing and lashing them, the blind boat was heading helplessly into the deep, deadly troughs of Lake Superior. The wheel was gone, stripped away with the pilot house, making the boat impossible to steer.

The mates, Captain Seph had instructed, would need to work like demons to fasten the couplings of the after wheel, a secondary, backup steering mechanism that could enable the master to regain control of his careening *Umbria*.

Mary McFadden stopped scribbling her notes and urged Cornaliusan to transport himself to that precise moment. The pump of memory didn't require much priming. He gushed with vivid descriptions of those decisive six minutes early in the *Umbria*'s forty-hour struggle.

Simply put, the second mate had been ready to die.

"I gave myself and the boat up for lost," he told McFadden in a halting voice. She, in turn, used shorthand to put it in her notebook, distracting from his story as little as possible.

"The sea was rolling fiercer than I had ever seen and, without the wheel, we were helpless in the trough of the sea. It was only the energy born of despair and the blind sense of duty that I sprang with the others to the after deck."

The ship rolled like a lumberjack's log as Cornaliusan and the first mate tried to set the couplings. "I never expected that we would live to see it done, for the ship was rolling horribly."

Three times, Cornaliusan was swept against the *Umbria*'s roped rails. "Freezing water, as it poured in torrents over me, nearly crushed my ribs."

Cornaliusan had been a deckhand, watchman, and mate on Great Lakes vessels since the early days of 1885. But he had never found himself in such desperate straits or amid such displays of bravery. As one man, his fate mattered little. But as part of a crew of twenty-two, Cornaliusan explained to McFadden, his adrenaline bubbled up as he tinkered with the after wheel's couplings.

"A hundred times while we struggled with the gearing, the hopelessness of the effort chilled my heart."

McFadden let his pause linger and stretch on uninterrupted.

"In my utter exhaustion, I cared little whether I went overboard or not. But the sight of those brave men made me ashamed of the feeling, for I knew they were all as hard bested as myself."

"Shame, then, in such critical moments, can be a powerful motivator?" McFadden asked. Cornaliusan nodded.

"The sight of a heroic deed takes the fear from the most cowardly heart, and certainly there was daring enough there in that hell of waters to make the boldest proud to be in such company."

Finally, Richardson and Cornaliusan succeeded in fastening the after-wheel couplings. The *Umbria* once again answered to its wheel. Cornaliusan told McFadden he was so weak and breathless by that point, he could only cling to the rail and wait for enough strength to crawl back to a more sheltered spot.

The next thirty-six hours, from one o'clock Tuesday morning to Wednesday night, were "like some horrid dream, for the apparently hopeless struggle was enough to daunt the bravest man."

The tears came fast now as the second mate gazed toward the passenger's cabin, where Captain Seph took refuge and now slept—his own cabin too flooded to occupy.

"Our captain, God bless him," Cornaliusan said. "If ever there was a man worth dying for, it's him, and every man jack of us will say the same."

So intently focused on note-taking, Mary McFadden hadn't realized that some dozen sailors were listening in on her interview with the second mate. But when the group suddenly roared in agreement with Cornaliusan's praise of their captain, even the timbers of the boat seemed to throb human-like, joining the unison of the sentiment.

Mary looked to the faces, cut, bruised, and pocked from the ordeal. Eyes glistened.

While shame may have played a role in the heroics, Mary intuited that loyalty, more so, underpinned all the endurance the men had displayed.

"A hundred times," Cornaliusan continued,

> the men were cheered by the noble words and example of the skipper, who, cool as a man at ease in his own home, kept constantly on the alert. There is not a man but felt that if consummate skill could save the ship, the captain was the man to do it, and no one can realize the value of this implicit confidence and the good it does a man in the face of death

unless he has passed through the deep waters and faced the grim monster as did the crew of the *Umbria*. No man could be anything but a hero under Captain Seph, and the result proved that our confidence in him was not mislaid. No man could think of despair while he was around, and despite the numbing cold and exhaustion of the struggle, not a man failed for a moment in his duty.

A Finnish watchman named Ellis Nyman came closest to death, Cornaliusan told McFadden. Numbed and stunned, he clung to the rope of the forward rail. Cornaliusan recalled how his fellow mate from Cleveland, Joe Richardson, realized Nyman's predicament and leaped through a swamping wave to grab the Finn and drag him back to the others. Just then, another billow broke over the deck. With an iron grip, Richardson held on to Nyman's collar with one hand and the rail with the other until the wave subsided.

Captain Seph and Mate Richardson were not the only heroes. Cornaliusan made sure Mary McFadden understood how the three Irish firemen shoveling coal down below—Joe Molloy of Cleveland, Patrick Murphy of Buffalo, and Edward Denison of Watertown, New York—labored until they needed to be carried from the hole more dead than alive.

In the next day's *News Tribune*, Mary McFadden would write: "They knew they might be engulfed at any moment and caught like rats in a trap. Yet they stuck to their posts and never for a moment let the steam go down a pound."

In his official report, Captain Seph detailed with little fanfare how the after-wheel steering was needed to get the *Umbria* to Grand Marais. After thirty-eight hours in the storm, the boat went forty miles, then hugged the North Shore down to Duluth. He estimated damage to the *Umbria* at $2,000.

"The sea was very rough," Seph concluded understatedly in the captain's report, "but the cargo was saved."

Before she left the boat to return to the newspaper office to file her report, Mary McFadden peeked in the passenger's cabin where Captain Seph slept. Cuts and bruises marked his face. She also noted that the wheelmen from Cleveland, Henry Larson and Edward Olson, needed to have both their feet and hands rubbed and rolled between warm blankets to thaw the extremities numbed during forty hours of brutal exposure.

"Yet so hardy are they that they are already up and around as if nothing had happened."

III

"As terrible as it is; as cruel and pathetic as it strikes home, it is the tragic story retold, and all who have known him in life know well that he met it without a quiver."

~ *Grand Haven Daily Tribune*
December 2, 1905

Five clusters of light on the Great Lakes shorelines. Five ports in the storm's aftermath: Ashland, Wisconsin; Two Harbors, Minnesota; Chicago, Illinois; Grand Haven, Michigan; and of course, Duluth, Minnesota.

The word spread between the cities by teletype, telephone, and, primarily, mouth. That Friday night, December 1, 1905, another powerful Pittsburgh Steamship, the 413-foot *Sir William Siemens*, limped into Ashland—some fifty miles overland from Duluth but twice that distance for boats because of the Apostle Islands sprinkled around the thumb of the Bayfield Peninsula jutting out of Wisconsin's northern tip.

Siemens Captain M. K. Chamberlain was quickly connected to Harry Coulby's post-storm vortex on the seventh floor of the Wolvin

The *Ira H. Owen*, pictured here amid Victorian fashion, was the center of tragedy during the Thanksgiving storm. *Historical Collections of the Great Lakes, Bowling Green State University*

Building. Chamberlain described an eerie and macabre scene he'd encountered on the slate water of Lake Superior, a dozen miles east of Michigan Island in the Apostles. At ten o'clock Friday morning, the *Siemens'* lookout spotted a mass of wreckage in the water. Twisted stairs, stanchions, and the top of a cabin drifted in the lake. Punctuating the wreckage, a dozen life preservers floated in the foam. They bore the name S.S. *Ira Owen*.

The *Owen* spilled out of the Globe Iron Works Company in Cleveland in 1877 with a steel hull and two boilers below, fueling a paltry 750-horsepower engine. Twin smokestacks topped the boat's stern. In the early years, the *Owen* hauled iron ore from Escanaba, Michigan, to south Chicago.

More than a quarter century later, the *Owen* was carrying 116,000 bushels of barley—a light load for a 262-foot freighter capable of moving 2,900 tons beneath its seven hatch coverings.

Alva Kellar knew the ship well. The captain of the *Harold B. Nye*, a three-year-old 380-footer, Kellar had left Duluth Harbor that Monday afternoon with his own load of grain about the same time as the *Owen*. By Friday night, Alva Kellar was in Two Harbors, having staggered into port drawing twenty-six feet of water forward.

Like Captain Chamberlain over in Ashland, Alva Kellar had a haunting tale to tell. He'd heard distress whistles blaring that Tuesday out on the eastern edge of the Apostles. The vessel, about forty miles off of Outer Island, looked to Kellar like a wooden boat, badly battered. Kellar doubted the ship, its distress whistles barking, could ride out the storm for long. Perhaps its load had shifted or the weather had caused something to go awfully awry.

In the blowing snow, Kellar lost sight of the wailing steamer not long after he caught a glimpse of it. Of course, he had a crew of his own to protect. And just about the time Kellar saw the injured boat, his mate, Bill Sturtevant, washed over near Outer Island, leaving a widow with two kids in Cleveland.

When the snow cleared a couple hours after Captain Kellar and the *Nye*'s crew had seen what they figured was the *Owen*, there was neither a boat in sight nor a whistle's blare shrieking across the water.

Kellar's belief that he had seen a wooden boat off Outer Island offered a wisp of hope. But could a captain, scrambling to keep his own boat afloat, really gauge the difference between a wooden hull and a steel steamer through thick snow? Kellar told the folks in Two Harbors, and Coulby and his people twenty-seven miles down in Duluth, that he was convinced he'd seen two stacks belching black smoke.

A couple of other twin stackers were operating that week in Duluth's harbor. But shipping records show the *Parks Foster*, the *Owen*'s sister ship and partner on all those iron ore runs from Escanaba, had left Duluth on Wednesday after the storm finally began to ease. The *Fred Mercur* also sported two smokestacks. But it was still loading grain in the harbor that Friday.

In Chicago, Captain J. J. Keith compared all the reports flowing into his office at the National Steamship Company—owners of the *Owen*. A veteran lake captain himself, Keith knew the distance was not great between Captain Kellar's sighting of the *Owen* off Outer Island and the lifejackets and wreckage Captain Chamberlain had discovered due south off Michigan Island.

As manager of National Steamship, Keith had been to Duluth a week earlier when his company's trusty old freighter, the *Ira H. Owen*, was waiting out the earlier storm. He'd spent three days in Duluth. He'd replaced hatch coverings, overhauling them so they'd be snug and seaworthy. He'd insured the twenty-seven-year-old boat for $100,000, and the cargo, as well, this being the end of November and all.

For the first few days, Keith felt confident the *Owen* was hiding on the lee side of one of the Apostles. Or that the lifeboats could have ferried some of the men to shelter. But as the hours crawled by, he acknowledged the inevitable and sent a dispatch from Chicago over the wire to Mary McFadden's newsroom and other Great Lakes newspapers:

"Why the steamer should have met disaster will always remain a mystery, I fear, for there is no hope that any of the crew are still alive."

That Saturday, Bill Loutit of Grand Haven, Michigan, used a series of long-distance telephone operators to connect with Captain Keith in

Chicago. Newspapers from Buffalo to Detroit to Chicago were reporting the wreckage Captain Chamberlain described in Ashland, Wisconsin. They also shared Captain Kellar's account of a twin stacker blowing distress whistles off Outer Island.

The first sketchy word that drifted back to Grand Haven—that Captain Honner had gone down with the ship—created a brief and heartbreaking misidentification. Most of the townsfolk thought Thomas Honner was still in town, not knowing he was filling in for a sick captain on a last November run. Everyone assumed Captain George Honner, Tom's brother, had drowned with the foundered boat. Lanterns swinging by their sides, the townsfolk came down the road to tell Aggie Honner she'd become a widow. But her husband, George, turned up in safe harbor in Marquette, Michigan, mastering the *Fleetwood*. The misinformation and confusion spread over two days.

Loutit, a bigwig in Grand Haven's small harbor, finally agreed to work the phone—no simple task with all the down lines still needing repair. Over a crackly connection from Chicago, Keith confirmed the ache in Grand Haven's collective gut. Loutit sent word to Elizabeth Honner, Thomas's wife of eleven years, and the kids, Thomas Junior, Doris, and little Bennie.

In that Saturday morning's *Grand Haven Daily Tribune*, the newspaper writer put it this way: "It was [of] the wife and little family and cozy home waiting impatiently to receive him when the voyage was ended that Captain Honner probably thought when the final summons came to him in the gale and storm and fury of Lake Superior, which he had met many times and vanquished many times before."

Seventy-five years before Thomas Honner's boat disappeared into the waves of Lake Superior, his father Edward Honner boarded a ship in Liverpool.

His clan had come from French blood. But his forebears, known as Honore, branched out to England, Ireland, and Australia. For many generations, Edward Honner's people had been planters in Ireland. He sailed for New York on March 23, 1830.

Why Edward Honner emigrated to America might be explained by the tense social conditions in Ireland, where gangs were hassling the Protestant gentry. More likely, though, his flight was prompted by the notion that he had inherited a large parcel of land in Lewis County in upstate New York near Utica. A relative named John Howard had fought for the British against the American revolutionaries, and this relative had apparently left him land.

When Edward Honner arrived some fifty years later, he found the title to the land defective. The Canadian Rebellion had men on both sides of the border fighting in 1837. And the Honners and Howards continually bounced across the border, seeking improved opportunities. Getting accurate land information back to Ireland, which was embroiled in its own chaos, apparently led to the title troubles.

It turned out that Howard had left New York for Canada and a plot of land the Crown deeded him. When Edward Honner and his brother William showed up on the boat from Liverpool, they found the strength of family ties far more solid than the flimsy title to the land they dreamed about in New York.

Thus began the Honners' rootless ways and frequent moves across the Canadian border. Edward only stayed in the young American republic for a few years before moving to Port Hope on the Canadian side of Lake Ontario.

Edward Honner's son Thomas was born in Cobourg, Ontario, on March 2, 1847. By the time Thomas Honner turned three, the family had settled in Amherstburg, just south of Windsor and across the Detroit River some eighteen miles south of Detroit.

An avid reader since boyhood, Thomas found the schools of Amherstburg unchallenging. His thirst for learning soon collided with the lure of Great Lakes sailing vessels. He juggled a couple terms at Oberlin College in Ohio as a teenager, by which time he had already started a regular rotation of work on schooners, barks, and tugs. His ship assignments carried a poetic ring.

From 1862 to 1864, Thomas Honner went before the masts of the schooners *Narragansett*, *Oneonta*, and *Saranac*. That third season, copper-hauling *Saranac* captain Charlie Gale hired Thomas to sail back to where his father had departed some three decades previously.

The ship reached Liverpool on July 4, 1864. By that fall, Thomas was working as a deckhand on a bark out of Buffalo, christened *Sunrise*. His seabag, increasingly filled with books and memories, was becoming well worn.

He hired on to the bark *Thermatis* and a schooner named *Oak Leaf* in the mid-1860s before becoming the wheelsman on Detroit River tugs *Prindiville* and *Castle*. By the time he turned twenty, Thomas Honner was climbing the ranks of the Alger tug fleet, towing rafts around Detroit.

On April 11, 1867, six weeks after his twenty-first birthday, Honner walked into the district court in Detroit, raised his right hand, denounced any allegiance to the queen of Great Britain and Ireland, and was sworn in as a U.S. citizen. He walked out of the courthouse and back to the docks, his mustache now thickening on the middle of his long watermelon of a face.

After two seasons as first mate of the tug *Torrent*, Thomas became a tug captain of the *Hector*, *Gladiator*, *Castle*, and *Wisconsin*. Like so many lake men, he would move from Amherstburg to Detroit to Kenosha, Wisconsin—where he married Elizabeth Duffy on May 8, 1894. As his family grew, so, too, did his reputation as a safe and reliable shipping master. He was hired promptly every spring and became one of the first members of the Buffalo Ship Masters' Union, Branch 6.

By April 1898, perhaps at Elizabeth's urgings or the pull of his three young children, Thomas Honner left the tug bridges and started working as a hull inspector for the U.S. Steamboat Inspector Service. For eight years, he checked hulls, sticking close to home and his family, which had settled back south of the border in Grand Haven, Michigan.

The itch became too much by 1904, and Thomas resigned his post as an inspector, giving up the paperwork for the helm of the *City of Straits*, a Hackley Line steamer that plowed back and forth on Lake Michigan between Muskegon and Chicago. By mid-November, he was back home with Elizabeth, little Thomas, Doris, and Bennie.

But his longtime peer, Captain J. J. Keith, manager of the National Steamship Company, needed an experienced skipper to take temporary command of the *Ira H. Owen*. When it came to veterans of Great Lakes shipping, Captain Joe Hulligan was as well-known as Thomas Honner. And he'd fallen sick. Keith convinced Honner that he would only be needed for one final run. He must have offered a handsome enough fee that Honner figured could help get his family through the long coming winter.

Truth be told, Thomas Honner didn't need much convincing. He'd crisscrossed the Great Lakes for forty-plus years. Being out on the Lakes, even in November, was where he belonged. Sure, he had a warm home in Grand Haven. But at fifty-eight, the Lakes were his true home and haven.

Captain Thomas Honner poses circa 1900 with his son, Thomas, and his daughter, Doris. The captain was convinced in November 1905 to take temporary command of the *Ira H. Owen* for a final run across the Lakes. *Courtesy of Tom Honore of Woolwine, Virginia, his grandson*

The *Grand Haven Daily Tribune* reflected the sentiment of the townsfolk, surrendering any optimism in Saturday's edition, on December 2, 1905:

> There seems to be no chance for a mite of hope. The steamer was in the open sea when last sighted and even if the crew could have left the ship in the boats there would be little chance for them in the terrible freezing weather which prevailed at the time. Everything seems to indicate that the ship foundered in the unequal fight against the sea.

If she had struck some of the islands there might be a bare chance of the crew being able to save themselves. But even the most optimistic hardly clutch at that straw and every marine man in the city and every person who knew Captain Honner is sorrow stricken and stunned by the terrible news of his probable fate.

The sympathy of the whole city is extended to his wife, whose anxious hours of the past few days have been a misery to her, only such a misery as can be experienced by the wife of a sailor. Hearts go out to his three little children, Thomas, Doris and little Bennie, who were the balm and value of the captain's life ashore. His wife and babies are fortunate that they may carry through the rest of their saddened lives, that they held and loved such a man as Captain Honner, among the bravest of the brave and the truest of the true. Captain Honner was rich in the regard and esteem of his townsmen and fellow mariners. His character was staunch and lasting. Sons, whose fathers loved him, bear that same deep regard for him. What more can a man wish for in life? What better memory can he leave behind?

Elizabeth Honner, Thomas' widow, delayed any talk of a memorial service. But after nine days filled with denial and defiance, she relented.

As preparations were being made, Elizabeth Honner received a letter addressed with a shaking hand.

It came from Charlie Gale, the old ship captain and Thomas Honner's mentor. He was ninety years old and stricken to his deathbed. It was Captain Gale who, in 1864, had hired Thomas Honner at seventeen years of age and sailed with him to Liverpool. Elizabeth Honner read the letter and made sure it was added to the program for the memorial service in Grand Haven:

> I knew Thomas Honner when he was a mere boy and am proud to say all he gave promise of then he has fulfilled in his after life. He sailed with me on the ocean (before the mast) and all through his life. It has seemed to me he has been the embodiment of all his own name implies. Honner by name and honor by nature. To you his chosen consort though we have never met, let me say, God keep you as you rear his children so they may leave such a heritage to their children as did he, that of an honored name. Teach them I pray you to live as he, 'with malice towards none and charity to all.'
>
> He has passed to his reward. I feel I will soon be with him in happy reunion. I should have been most pleased if God had so ordered to have met you. I would have been glad indeed to have held the children of Thomas Honner in my trembling old arms. I have been a life long friend of their family. . . . I am

slipping away fast and I hope that I who led this young man to the sea may meet him and have him guide me when life's tempestuous storm is o'er and that he will safely pilot me to that home of safety which he has found.

Write me my dear, Mrs. Honner. With love to your children and self, I am while life lasts, your friend, CHAS. GALE.

Captain Gale died that winter, a few weeks after sending the letter, which included this little verse:

'Tis hard dear one to part with thee,
We'll meet on earth no more:
Your happy home will never be
Just as it was before.

They'll miss you there, the years around
Will be desolate and drear:
Your vacant chair the sad waves sound,
Tells the tale:—you are not here.

Yet we will not grieve—we should not grieve
For you loved one, from this earth fled:
No tear should start, no sigh should heave,
For you we love, whom we call dead.

Though from our side loved ones be riven,

They are not dead who dwell in heaven:

Faith views them in that land of bliss,

In visions calm and even:

Where souls in sympathy unite

A family in heaven.

IV

"There are sailors living today who went through the

1905 blow who will tell you that it is the worst ever to

occur on the Great Lakes. . . . The old-timers will tell

you that the 1905 blow had more snow, wind and

seas than anything yet seen."

~ Dana Thomas Bowen
Memories of the Lakes, 1945

Harry Coulby could take it no longer. For days now, he had paced the seventh floor of the Wolvin Building, chewing his cigars until they were frayed and soggy. Ten of his Pittsburgh Steamships had been battered and damaged. None were insured. Coulby had stubbornly balked at paying the stiff premiums, roughly $20,000 for each new ore vessel.

A dozen of his sailors were dead, nine of them frozen or washed off the *Mataafa*, which sat crippled and cracked in the ice for everyone in Duluth to see and ponder. All told, nearly thirty Great Lakes ships had been ravaged on the western half of Lake Superior alone. The *Ira Owen* had foundered with Captain Thomas Honner and eighteen others aboard. Seventeen ships had been stranded, and about a dozen others were damaged.

Harry Coulby had to get out of the office. The young giant of Great Lakes shipping needed the fresh, cold air and the spray of the waves. The numbers being tallied made his head ache. Not far inside the Duluth Ship Canal, the 5,165-ton *Isaac L. Ellwood*, crammed with ore, had settled in twenty-two feet of water after ramming the piers. Salvagers told Coulby he was looking at a $50,000 repair bill on the *Ellwood* alone.

Up near the cliffs of Gold and Split Rock, Coulby's *Madeira* barge had splintered and sank—a $175,000 loss. It would cost $50,000 to pry loose from the rocky shore its consort steamer, the 436-foot, 5,309-ton *Edenborn*, and make it seaworthy again. On the eastern side of Keweenaw Point, Coulby learned from a telegram, the 413-foot *Coralia* and its barge *Maia* had smashed into the shore but shouldn't cost too much to float again.

Yet of all the Pittsburgh Silver Stackers strewn up and down the North Shore and the South Shore of Lake Superior, Harry Coulby felt most shaken by the stranding of the *William E. Corey*. After all, this monster was named after Coulby's brother in industry, the new president of U.S. Steel, Bill Corey.

At a whopping 558 feet long and nearly 6,500 tons, the *Corey* was Coulby's flagship. Granted, it was one of four new Pittsburgh Steamship bulk freights put into service in June 1905, just six months earlier. But unlike the *Gary* and the two others, the *Corey* came equipped with sumptuous staterooms for entertaining executives and cronies of U.S. Steel's wealthy rulers. Each room had a private bathtub and was awash in birch and enameled white paint. A guest dining room and observation deck added to the *Corey*'s swagger. When it launched, Coulby chartered trains to carry three thousand people from Chicago's LaSalle Street Station to the Chicago Shipbuilding Company's yards.

Bill Corey himself was traveling in Europe, so he sent his sister, Ada, to join Coulby for all the festivities. Men in straw hats and women decked in Victorian finery watched Ada christen her brother's namesake in the grimy old shipyard. The whole crowd then crammed into a banquet hall rented out at the Chicago Auditorium. Coulby sat with his old predecessor, Augustus Wolvin, who was toasted as "the man who built the first leviathan on the lakes."

Coulby's daydream ended with some Lake Superior spray nearly six months later on the eastern side of the Apostles. He was sailing out to oversee the salvage of the *Corey*, which had snagged seeking shelter from the storm behind Michigan Island. The crewmembers had held on through a long night of massive combers—and survived. But their boat was now caught on Gull Island Reef, exposed and vulnerable despite its massive size. It wasn't too far from where the *Owen* and Captain Thomas Honner had disappeared.

Coulby's insistence on supervising the *Corey*'s salvage bordered on obsession. He ordered a small armada to perform the task. He contracted a trio of tugs: the *Crosby*, the *Edna G.*, and Honner's old charge, the *Gladiator*. But that was just the start. Coulby himself joined *Mariposa* skipper Bill Reed, whom he considered the company's sharpest salvager. He signed up two other bulk freights of the Pittsburgh fleet, the *Manola* and the *Marina*, to join the team, along with a couple 400-footers, the *Douglass Houghton* and the *William Siemens*. For the *Siemens*, the mission brought a scaled-down crew back to the nightmare of wreckage from the *Owen* they had sailed through a week earlier.

As Coulby barked orders, gobbled cigars, and watched salvage crews try to loosen the *Corey* from its underwater snare, he couldn't help but chuckle at the irony. Here was the 282-foot *Manola*, built fifteen years earlier with a triple expansion engine. When it spilled from the yard in

1890, the *Manola* had been the queen of the Minnesota Steamship fleet. It could haul 68,000 tons of ore in one season. Now it was groaning and pulling the *Corey*, which was twice as long and could carry 225,000 tons of ore per year, or four times the freight. The triple expansion engines and boiler rooms were the same size, but due to improvements in efficiency the new boats had nearly twice the horsepower. Yet the old boat was pulling the new, longer, wider freighter. Coulby shrugged off any notion that the new boats were oversized for their engines. It wasn't his nature to consider marching too fast in his attempts to expand the capacity, efficiency, and profitability of his massive fleet.

It took a dozen days and some hull-scraping damage to the *William Siemens* and the little tug *Edna G.*, but on December 10, 1905, Coulby's navy finally succeeded in prying the $450,000 *William E. Corey* loose. The steamers *Houghton* and *Marina* were the vessels to pull it free of the rocks.

The sailors shouted when the big boat started floating again in the cold green water. Coulby smiled, too, even though the *Corey* would require a $100,000 overhaul back at the Chicago shipyards. The crew was safe and the flagship was sailing again.

IV

"Porphyry and Greenstone, the latter much disturbs the Compass Needle. The depth of Water everywhere too great for a Vessel to anchor."

~ Canadian Lieutenant Henry Bayfield's
chart of the North Shore, 1825

Once the *Corey* had been yanked from the rocks of the Apostle Islands, Harry Coulby returned to Cleveland on his private train, cutting through the cold darkness of a December night.

The season had been a debacle. The unexpected storms in September and October were bad enough, only to be followed by the worst storm anyone had ever seen. The crew of the *Owen* and the nine men killed on the *Mataafa* expanded the long list of dead sailors. Counting routine collisions and accidents, more than one hundred men had died that autumn and more than two hundred deaths were reported for the season across all five Lakes.

Harry Coulby came up with his response in the smoky haze of his sleeper car, rattling through Wisconsin and around the southern tip of Lake Michigan. He forgot about the hidden reefs that snared the *Corey*. Thick eyebrows scrunched, Coulby focused his attention back to Lake Superior's North Shore. He'd been out on a tug to see where his barge, the *Madeira*, had splintered and sunk. He'd surveyed the *Edenborn* nearby and then sailed a dozen miles southwest to the twisted wreckage of the *Lafayette*. Only its stern could be salvaged.

Coulby puffed his cigar and grabbed a pencil and a scratch of paper. His arithmetic was jolted by the jostling of the train and the huge numbers:

Lafayette $300,000
Madeira. $175,000
Edenborn $100,000
$575,000

More than a half-million dollars had been lost on a rocky stretch of Minnesota's North Shore twenty miles north of Two Harbors and some fifty miles above Duluth.

Back in 1854, a surveyor named Thomas Clark had identified a sheer cliff promontory called Stony Point in his journal as "good for a lighthouse." Others called the site Split Rock. A river by that name, christened by Canadian officer Henry Bayfield in 1825, split the rock canyon a couple miles southeast of Clark's Stony Point.

Now Harry Coulby would make his mark on the rocky cliff that had snared four of his boats. He knew the Pittsburgh Steamship Company had to be aggressive. Storms had dented his merged corporation's expansionist vision—but not its spirit.

In an idea hatched in his smoky chartered train car, Harry Coulby organized his brothers of lake commerce, the Lake Carriers' Association, an ownership cartel controlling some five hundred bulk freighters. They in turn petitioned their ship captains. Coulby and his fellow shipping titan, Cleveland lawyer Harvey Goulder, descended on Washington for some strong-arm lobbying and cigars and brandy.

Lighthouses. That's what Coulby demanded to counter the destructive storms. Lots of new lighthouses—especially one equipped with a fog whistle near the stony point known as Split Rock.

America was growing. Ships were growing. Industry was growing. Profits were growing. And no rocky coastline was going to threaten all that. Besides, Harry Coulby liked the metaphor of a lighthouse, a beacon in the darkness, set high on a rock ledge, guiding progress forward.

He saw himself as a kind of lighthouse of commerce. And he knew he had to offer some sort of response to the horrors of the shipping season. Pushing for new lighthouses—a half-million dollars of new lighthouses on the Great Lakes alone—topped his list of demands.

Eighty-five ship masters signed his petition, requesting a light and fog signal at Split Rock. The Lake Carriers' Association unanimously backed the effort. Coulby's argument needed to be convincing. He pointed out that ore deposits in the area screwed up captains' compasses. The dramatic drop in depths off the North Shore made sound readings pointless. More than a half million dollars had been squandered on these rocks, Coulby told the politicians in Washington.

The lives lost seldom came up in the conversations; it wasn't part of the rhetoric.

"It was the destiny of the United States to become the imperial factor in iron and steel and in industrial pursuits," Coulby's sidekick, Harvey Goulder, repeated in his speeches. "The destiny of the United States has never been halted for the lack of human instruments."

Coulby and Goulder joked with lawmakers that Lake Superior was "a boy growing out his clothes."

They were convincing, if not a bit misleading. The talk of imperialism and destiny and industrial pursuits eclipsed the practical reality. Simply put, a light and fog signal at Split Rock was a kneejerk response to a nightmarish autumn of storms. Had the lighthouse been erected by 1904, instead of in 1910, experts doubt it would have made much difference to the *Madeira*, *Edenborn*, *Layfayette*, or its barge, the *Manila*. The ships likely would have found the same fate on the rocks. Lost in the windy proclamations of Coulby and his cohorts was an Eleventh District office report to the Lighthouse Board in Washington:

"It is not . . . obvious what service a light at Split Rock can perform." The report suggested that, in clear weather, a lighthouse was unnecessary to navigate the forty-five-mile run from Devil's Island in the Apostle Islands to the foghorn- and light-equipped port of Two Harbors, Minnesota. During thick weather, the light in Two Harbors alerted captains to the coastline and the adjoining fog whistle "is amply sufficient for the guidance of vessels."

Shipping practices of the era's iron ore trade, the report noted, called for running at full speed in all weather. "But for this feature of present practice, there would be no need of either a light or fog signal near Split Rock Point."

The message from Cleveland, on the other hand, had been clear. Full speed ahead. Had the ships been allowed to ease across the water from the Apostles to Minnesota's North Shore, a lighthouse would never have been constructed. But the water was deep and the compass unreliable, Coulby maintained, disguising the real reason behind the Split Rock Lighthouse. Preventing shipwrecks sounded good. But the report from the Eleventh District of the U.S. Lighthouse Board made the real motivation clear:

"Of greater importance than the number of wrecks is, however, the fact that in the absence of a fog signal at Split Rock, vessels are greatly delayed in making Two Harbors, and because of the large number of vessels involved, the money loss due to this delay must be very considerable."

Harry Coulby had no time for delays. Enough money had been wasted. They needed lighthouses, especially at Split Rock. Legislation was drafted. Knute Nelson of Minnesota carried the bill in the U.S. Senate, and Theodore E. Burton of Cleveland led the charge in the

House of Representatives. By March 1907, the bill had sailed through the United States Congress, appropriating $75,000 for a lighthouse and fog signal to be constructed at Split Rock. The money was part of a $500,000 package to build lighthouses on the Great Lakes.

Through tricky construction, using barges and hoists, a blond brick lighthouse and keepers' quarters rose near the cliff where Fred Benson had once scrambled up, squirrel-like, with a rope in his hands and freezing waves lashing his back. The stone sentinel blinked through the fog and snow for decades before becoming a hot stop for tourists careening up the North Shore.

Perched on its cliff top, 178 feet high, Split Rock Lighthouse became a lasting legacy of Fred Benson's desperate climb, Harry Coulby's impatience for delays, and 1905's three-day blow on Minnesota's rockbound North Shore.

The wreck of the *Madeira* prompted Congress to appropriate the funds for Split Rock Lighthouse, which was erected near where the barge sank. Some argue it wouldn't have helped much in the 1905 storm. *Minnesota Historical Society*

PART 5

I
_____

A shipwreck,
The wild waters roar and heave.
The brave vessel is dashed all to pieces,
And all the helpless souls within her drowned;
All save one.
A man whose soul is greater than the tempest
And his spirit stronger than the sea's embrace.
Not for him a watery end, but a new life
Beginning on a stranger shore.

> ~ William Shakespeare, *The Tempest*

"Old men look back upon what they did, when
young, when everything is measured by the
magnified prowess of their own youth."

> ~ Duluth admiralty lawyer Henry Ransom Spencer
> Appeals brief, May 24, 1909

On the spring day of May 18, 1918, off the coast of France, a German submarine unleashed a torpedo. It hummed below the saltwater waves before tearing a massive hole in the steel plates of the *S. C. Reynolds*. The 255-foot, twenty-eight-year-old cargo ship sank on the spot.

Thirteen years earlier, the *Reynolds* had arrived in Duluth's harbor at four o'clock on a Monday afternoon, just as a three-day storm was beginning to blow—what would come to be known as the *Mataafa* Blow. Stevedores unloaded the cargo as the dockhands tied the *Reynolds* way out at the end of the city dock. From five o'clock until about ten thirty that night—with an hour break for supper—the unloading continued and the weather worsened. Captain Herrick signaled for the Union tugboats to help him depart, but they refused. The danger was too great for any vessel, even tugs, to leave the port. So the crew of the *Reynolds* replaced the chafed ropes, knowing if the steel freighter broke loose, it would likely smash into another boat in the wave-swept harbor. A day later, when the storm eased up a bit, the *Reynolds* sailed downbound to Lake Erie for winter layup. As the boat pulled away from Duluth, it become quickly clear that the night of relentless pounding had left the city dock damaged.

Lillian Kelly and R. C. Vincent owned the dock and knew some lawyers. They filed a lawsuit in state court against the Lake Erie Transportation Company, which owned the *Reynolds*. They asked for $1,200 in damages.

The three-day storm of 1905 left many legacies—from construction of Split Rock Lighthouse to the practice of placing bow-to-stern cables on freighter decks. That could have saved the frozen men who resisted sprinting from the aft of the *Mataafa* to the warmth of the forecastle. Captain McLennan of the Life-Saving Service, on orders from Washington, began placing his lifeboats on both sides of Duluth's jutting canal piers.

For law students, though, the case of *Vincent v. Lake Erie Transportation Company* became a famous legal squabble and mainstay in leading casebooks. A Minnesota Supreme Court opinion defined the complex rules about liability for harm caused by necessity. When one party, in this case the *Reynolds*, uses another's property for his benefit, he's liable for any harm done whether it's his fault or not.

A dozen men sat on the jury in September 1908, as Judge Josiah Ensign refereed the jousting of two of Duluth's sharpest legal minds. Both were former Minnesota legislators down in St. Paul. Admiralty lawyer Henry Ransom Spencer defended the ship owners, while E. F. Alford argued for the dock owners, calling witnesses to attest to the damage caused by the *Reynold's* tie-up. Because the captain had chosen to replace the ropes and keep the ship on the dock, Alford argued, the damage was a deliberate outcome, not some inevitable accident. Never mind that untethering from the dock in the midst of a gale might have destroyed the boat or other vessels in the harbor.

The ship's lawyer sat down with Duluth meteorologist Herbert Richardson for a pre-trial deposition. His meticulous weather records became exhibits in the trial. Richardson testified that storm warnings had been issued at ten o'clock that Monday morning and published in the afternoon paper. He explained how the wind was blowing less than 20 miles per hour at noon, increasing to 34 miles per hour by five o'clock that evening when the *Reynolds* arrived.

Snow began to fall at 6:30 p.m., and wind speeds between 54 and 62 miles per hour were recorded until midnight. The wind was blowing up to 68 miles per hours by eight the next morning. The attorneys clashed over whether the ship captain was negligent for docking up far from safety with warning flags out, or whether the dock owners were just as much to blame for having their hands direct the *Reynolds* to the end of the dock.

After a three-day trial, the jury came up with a compromise verdict and ordered the ship owners to fork over $500 for the damage to the dock. On a 3-2 vote in the winter of 1910, the Minnesota Supreme Court agreed. A newly appointed justice named Thomas Dillon O'Brien wrote the majority opinion, comparing the case to a starving man who takes food from another to save his life. Surely, that man would be obliged to repay the food costs if he were later able. If such moral obligation applies, O'Brien argued, then so, too, should the legal obligation. The case, destined to become famous in legal circles, garnered little attention in Duluth's newspapers. They mentioned the case in the court calendar and didn't publish a word on the Supreme Court's ruling. The *Harvard* and *Columbia Law Reviews* promptly picked up on the case. For nearly a century, the case has been cited in countless cases and analyzed by legal scholars.

Many compared the case to the hypothetical dilemma of an unprepared hiker caught by surprise in a fierce storm. The hiker finds an unoccupied cabin, where he burns wood and eats food to survive. All agree the hiker acted reasonably and out of necessity. Had the cabin owner been around, he would have been morally obligated to welcome the hiker with food and warmth at no cost. But the cabin owner wasn't there, and the hiker had not offered to repay the costs of the food and wood.

As law professors are wont to ask, does the hiker have a moral duty to repay and, if so, is he legally liable if the cabin owner sued for his losses? It is then that the law professors, in dusty shafts of sunlight, tell the story of the *S. C. Reynolds* and its crew tying up to the Duluth city dock on November 27, 1905.

The Lake Erie Transportation Company eventually sold the *Reynolds*, which was resold a couple times and rebuilt for ocean service in 1915. Three years later, the German torpedo sent the *Reynolds* to the sea bottom.

II

"Mary, like all of her sex, gets the pouts now and then and quits and then when she gets over bein' mad, she gathers up the shears, paste-pot and pencil and begins grinding out better stuff than ever . . . . "

~ Yellowed clipping from the *Duluth News Tribune*,
found in Mary McFadden's purse,
stolen July 31, 1909

In 1989, a young woman named Tracy Hunter was living behind a mansion in a old carriage-house apartment. The mansion had once been the residence of mining heiress Patsy Clark.

A couple of rowdy kids knocked a hole in the second-floor wall of the carriage house. And Hunter's cat, Gwendolyn, crawled on through. The search was on.

When her cat wouldn't respond to her pleas, Hunter knocked away some more of the plaster and went into the darkness, trembling with fear. She took shallow breaths and waited for something to leap out at her in horror-movie fashion. Some thirty feet inside the cramped space behind the wall, Hunter noticed a black object wedged between a chimney and a wall. At first, she thought it was a book. Then she realized it was a purse—an artificial leather square purse about eight inches by eight inches with a broken shoulder strap.

It was also a time capsule, a flashback satchel that dropped Hunter in 1909, when a newspaper reporter named Mary D. McFadden had put her purse down. Just for an instant. When Hunter unsnapped the center section of the purse, she found that any money or valuables it once contained had been plundered. A butler or maid must have snatched the purse, grabbed anything worth grabbing, and tucked it behind the chimney, where it would sit, forgotten and overlooked for eighty years—much like Mary McFadden herself.

The purse bulged with clues about McFadden. There was a $45 deposit slip from the City National Bank in Duluth and a series of yellowed newspaper clippings and notes scratched on a Great Northern Railroad conductor's delay reports.

Since her last interview with *Mataafa* Captain Dick Humble following the deadly 1905 storm, McFadden's reputation had only grown. She became a powerful voice on the editorial pages, lobbying for a tonnage tax to share some of the spoils of the wealthy mining barons. She became a leading force in the Minnesota suffrage struggle. And her poetry had become as popular as her zinging opinion pieces.

One of the old clippings in the purse, from an impossible-to-identify newspaper, had clearly made her proud enough to carry around:

> Whenever Miss McFadden is not on the job at the *News Tribune* office, the editorial page is as even as bread without salt and there has been nothing saline about it lately.

> This little lady was the life and light of that excellent
> paper. She was not only brilliant but original and intelligent. A
> newspaper woman that's a right good fellow is a scarcity in the
> business and Mary fills the bill.

By 1909, at the height of her career as a journalist and feisty suffragist, McFadden had hitched on as a correspondent with the *St. Paul Pioneer Press and Dispatch*. She had built a friendly and supportive relationship with John Johnson, Minnesota's charismatic Democratic governor. He was toying with a presidential campaign challenge to unseat William Taft in the 1912 election. (An academic fellow named Woodrow Wilson wound up winning.)

During the summer of 1909, Johnson tested the waters by booking a Great Northern train as part of a forty-four-guest gubernatorial entourage. They were bound for Washington State and the Alaska-Yukon-Pacific Exposition. A special Minnesota Day was on the schedule, complete with an unveiling of a bust of Great Northern railroad magnate and St. Paul icon James J. Hill.

McFadden sent dispatches to St. Paul and orchestrated the pomp, hype, and spin of the Minnesota delegation. Naturally, she found it easy to confide to her fellow journalists at the *Spokane-Review* the true nature of this juggernaut.

"That the present western tour of Governor Johnson is nothing less than a presidential boom under cover is declared by one of the party 'in' on the situation as it affects the Minnesota chief executive," the newspaper reported breathlessly, in two thirty-plus-word sentences. "This person 'in' on the situation is Mary McFadden, a political journalist who has studied the political situation in the Gopher state for a number of years and is a recognized authority."

McFadden was no doubt letting the Spokane reporters "in" when the governor's party came calling at one of the city's more prestigious mansions, belonging to mining mogul Patsy Clark. Whoever snatched her purse would ransack it and hide it out in the second floor of the carriage house. And there it would sit for eighty years until Tracy Hunter went nervously hunting for her cat, Gwendolyn.

Mary McFadden's purse contained telegrams from her St. Paul editors—along with antiperspirant face cream, a couple calling cards, pencils, and the latest from the *Political Equality Series* monthly newsletter from the American Women's Suffrage Association.

There was another faded clipping, too, pertaining to her on-again, off-again employment by the *Duluth News Tribune*:

"It is reported that Mary McFadden has resigned her position on the *Duluth News Tribune* staff, again, and that she will leave the state. Don't believe it. Mary, like all of her sex, gets the pouts now and then and quits and then, when she's over bein' mad, she gathers up the shears, paste-pot and pencil and begins grinding out better stuff than ever."

The prediction was right and wrong. She would remain in Duluth until 1914. When her lobbying for suffrage finally succeeded and Minnesota women were allowed to vote in 1920, McFadden was long gone. She had moved to New York City's Greenwich Village and roared her way into the 1920s, writing poetry, freelancing for magazines, and surrounding herself with the literati at the Algonquin's fabled roundtable.

Tracy Hunter tracked down one of McFadden's nieces. And Patricia Partridge, whose father was Mary's youngest brother, filled in some of the blanks. Mary had never married. The oldest of thirteen children, Mary McFadden's family tree was blessed with durable bark.

Her grandfather, Manus McFadden, died in 1929 in County Donegal, Ireland. He was 105 years old. His son, a hard-drinking carpenter named David McFadden, had fled the potato famine for New Brunswick, Canada, before drifting to tiny Graceville, Minnesota, on the state's western edge. He died in Montana at 94.

His wife, Julia, wasn't as lucky. She died in childbirth along with her thirteenth baby in Graceville in 1891. By then, Mary McFadden was seventeen years old and, as the oldest child, was forced to raise her siblings. Perhaps that experience doused her interest in rearing children of her own.

McFadden eventually made her way down to the University of Minnesota, hired on with the *Minneapolis Times* and, by 1903, had embarked on her decade as Duluth's first full-time woman journalist. Her coverage of the 1905 storm cemented her reputation as a compassionate, dramatic voice and spinner of human yarns. It also enhanced her disdain for the shipping giants, whose tonnage she urged should be taxed at a fair and steep rate.

Mary McFadden's trip to Spokane came at the precise midpoint of her life, when she was thirty-five years old. She spent her last thirty years in New York but decided to escape the bluster of the city in the spring of 1944. She headed out to Grangeville, Idaho, to visit her sister, Kate. She died of a heart attack at her sister's home at age seventy.

II

"Mr. Coulby would keep the trees in front of the house trimmed so he could watch his ships sailing by on Lake Erie."

~ Website of the City of Wickliffe, Ohio

The year after the Thanksgiving storm, as Harry Coulby began lobbying for a new lighthouse fifty miles north of Duluth, he apparently had no concerns that the big ore ships had outsized their overworked engines and contributed to all the tragedy.

Pittsburgh Steamship Company President Harry Coulby (*top row, second from right*) stands out in his English derby and natty attire at a 1919 lock opening. *Photo courtesy of Al Miller*

It was his third year as president and general manager of the gargantuan Pittsburgh Steamship Company, and Coulby placed orders for five new ships to be built at the Chicago Shipbuilding Company. They would all be 605 feet long, 58 feet wide, and 32 feet deep—36 feet longer than the *William E. Corey* he watched get wrenched off the Apostle Islands the previous December. The *Corey* was nine feet longer than the previous queen of the Lakes: the 560-foot *Augustus B. Wolvin*, named after his friend and predecessor.

Coulby named the first of his new 605-footers after J. Pierpoint Morgan, the financier behind U.S. Steel.

"Running expenses of these very large carriers were very little more than those of older boats and they carried practically the same sized crew. The engines also remain practically unchanged," Coulby's Lake Carriers' Association boasted in its 1910 annual report. That report included a lengthy "History of the Iron Ore Trade," something its authors said was important "in order that future generations may have a historical reference."

The treatise went on to brag that the ships built in 1905 and 1906, including the *Corey* and the *Morgan*, could haul ten thousand tons of ore—more than tripling the capacity of the 1888 boats that could carry closer to three thousand tons. "In comparison to their size, these bulk freighters are obviously of very low power, but nevertheless sufficient for the purpose," the report stated with both pride and callousness.

In 1913, Coulby celebrated his tenth year at the helm of the Pittsburgh Steamship Company by plucking down $1 million to build a mansion. It sat on fifty-four acres just outside Cleveland in the tiny unincorporated precinct of Wickliffe, in Willoughby Township. Coulby's handpicked architect, Frederick Striebinger, designed a sixteen-room palace with seven fireplaces, a Tiffany skylight, and hand-carved details. White-glazed terra cotta, imported from Italy, covered the exterior. The house took two years to construct.

Called Coulallenby, the mansion grounds encompassed formal gardens, a pond, a cow barn, and a gatehouse. A wrought iron fence and stone pillars surrounded the property.

The living room featured Tiffany chandeliers, carved cabinets, three Palladian windows, and a fireplace of imported Italian marble. Coulby's adjacent library had hand-carved panels from Bohemia, a view of the estate, and a hidden wall safe. Coulby's wife had her own bedroom, dressing room, sitting room, and private bath. Coulby's own bedroom upstairs in the east wing offered a view, over the trimmed trees, of ships sailing on Lake Erie. It had been thirty years since he had tried to hire on to the Lake Erie steamer *Onoko*, only to be turned down because of a lack of experience.

In 1916 Wickliffe's residents filed a petition asking permission to incorporate as a village. When the vote carried, Coulby was elected Wickliffe's first mayor.

After twenty years atop Pittsburgh Steamship Company, Coulby retired in 1924, shortly after his wife's death. He wanted to slow down and travel, although he remained involved as a partner at Pickands Mather and Company. He also stayed on as a member of the board of Central Alloy Steel Corporation, president of Interlake Steamship Company, and a director of Youngstown Sheet and Tube Company.

On December 10, 1928, Coulby embarked on an ocean cruise to England. He was spending the Christmas holidays with his sister, Lucy, in Claypole, Lincolnshire, and his brothers, William and Robert, in Newark, Nottingham. He had sailed full circle, returning to the cobblestone streets and stone-fenced farms of his childhood.

Coulby's valet found him dead in the Ritz Hotel in London on January 18, 1929. He was sixty-four. He was supposed to be on his way back to Wickliffe with a scheduled stop first in the West Indies. As a teenager, he'd gone to Cuba to work the telegraphs and hated it, stowing away to New York. Something lured him to return. But he wouldn't make the trip this time.

Coulby was buried in his family plot in the St. Peters Church yard in Claypole, Lincolnshire. He had bought the church new oak pews four years earlier, the same time he paid for the village hall and rebuilt the local school.

In 1951, Wickliffe's population grew to 5,002, making it a city. Within three years, city leaders negotiated a deal with Harry Coulby's estate to turn his mansion into City Hall. The west wing of the massive home, with the hand-carved wooden moldings and Tiffany chandeliers, became the City Council chambers. Coulby's library housed the office of his successor, serving as the mayor's office. The police department moved into the east wing's old dining room, breakfast nook, butler's pantry, and kitchen.

Although the mansion-to-City Hall deal came twenty-five years after Coulby's death, his estate drove a hard bargain. In exchange for the sumptuous castle and grounds, the city of Wickliffe had to hand over its old village hall, a fourteen-acre park on Bishop Road, and $70,000 in cash to Coulby's estate.

In his will, Coulby left $3 million to the Cleveland Foundation, a gift worth about $50 million in today's dollars. The money financed healthcare grants and was earmarked for needy youth—much like the eighteen-year-old Coulby who had lain ill in a New York charity hospital with malaria.

Two years before his death, Coulby watched the launching of the largest straight-deck bulk freighter from the American Ship Building Company's yard in Lorain, Ohio. The 631-foot *Harry Coulby* could carry 16,000 tons in four holds fed by eighteen hatches. It included ornate guest quarters and carried 14,650 tons of coal from Lorain to Duluth on its maiden trip in September, 1927. It returned with a U.S. carrier record of 13,731 tons of iron ore—a benchmark it would continually eclipse for fifteen years.

On July 1, 1940, the *Harry Coulby* became the first Great Lakes vessel to carry more than 16,000 tons of iron ore. When the St. Lawrence Seaway System opened in 1959, the *Coulby* sailed to the Canadian Gulf of St. Lawrence ports to obtain iron ore when U.S. Steel workers were on strike. If Coulby were looking down on his namesake, it's hard to say which he'd be prouder of: the record-breaking ore load or the strike-breaking voyage.

In the 1960s, the *Coulby* grounded in heavy fog and rammed a dock at Taconite Harbor, battering its bow. By 1980, with the shipping business in a downturn, the big boat carried only the occasional load of grain and was in long-term layup in Duluth.

The *Coulby* was rechristened the *Kinsman Enterprise* in 1989, a name given to honor an old ship controlled by the family of New York Yankees owner George Steinbrenner. In the fall of 2002, in Port Colborne, Ontario, the big old boat was sold for scrap.

IV

"Of course this locality has some disagreeable weather now and then. What place does not?"

~ Herbert Willard Richardson, 1914

A couple of years after Harry Coulby died, Herbert Willard Richardson did what he had done nearly every day for thirty-three years. He predicted Duluth's weather from his white house on the hill between Seventh and Eighth Streets near the Incline Railway's hilltop station. The home had doubled as the U.S. Weather Station since he designed the place in 1904.

On March 29, 1931, Richardson foresaw a chance of spring snow with winds fresh to strong coming down from the north. A few hours after filing that weather forecast, Richardson died at 8:30 that night. His death certificate listed several illnesses, ranging from pancreatic cancer to pneumonia to a perforated ulcer to gland problems. He was sixty-four.

Despite his many maladies, Richardson had continued to forecast the weather, save for a two-week span the previous winter when his pain was too severe.

The story of Richardson's death made front-page news in the *Duluth News Tribune*. His Pilgrim ancestors' arrival in 1620 was celebrated, as were his forebears' antics in the Mexican and Civil wars. Richardson had given up a reporter job at a newspaper in Alliance, Ohio, to join the weather bureau's precursor, the U.S. Army Signal Corps. That was in 1886 when he was nineteen years old. He came to Duluth in 1898.

His many writings, including the 1914 *The Climate of Duluth*, reflected his optimistic bent, his precision, and his steadfast devotion to Duluth:

"Some of our people have perhaps been too prone to dwell upon the unpleasant weather features of our climate. When we do have a storm or cold wave of any special consequence the fact has been advertised far and wide. It is the exceptional that excites comment, and particularly newspaper comment. The average excellence of the climate is accepted as a matter of course."

He always considered "the most severe local storm of record (as regards continuity and effects) . . . the northeaster and snow storm on November 27–28, 1905."

Among his weather facts, Richardson noted that the month following the big storm—December 1905—featured the lowest precipitation (0.07 inches) in his fat monthly record book.

He calculated the storm's average wind velocities at 42 miles per hour for twenty-nine hours, 50 to 60 miles per hour for fifteen hours, and rates of 60 miles per hour for thirteen hours with a maximum rate for any five-minute period of 68 miles per hour. "No other local storm has ever approached this one as to continuity."

And Herbert Richardson knew a thing or two about continuity. Aside from the weather, Richardson developed sizable expertise in the area of transporting perishable food. He blended his love of meteorology and backyard gardening. He wrote articles detailing how, to combat the high cost of living, he averaged fifteen bushels of potatoes a year from his 14×75–foot patch.

In the end, he was a booster, as a member of the Chamber of Commerce, the Engineers Club, and, of course, the Masonic orders. He was the past master and potentate of the Ionic Lodge and Aad Temple of the Mystic Shrine.

"His ability to express his thoughts in vivid and pleasing language, and his faithful, careful work, together with his kind and cheerful personality fitted him to an unusual degree for this sometimes trying position," according to the obituary in the May 1931 newsletter of the Minnesota Federation of Architects and Engineers.

"Loyal, faithful, diplomatic, energetic, accurate, all are terms that apply to his character. His keen sense of humor and his ready wit were also characteristics that endeared him to his friends. The engineering profession has lost a member of great worth and ability, the Head of the Lakes a loyal patriotic citizen and his family a devoted husband and father."

Funeral services for Richardson were held at the Masonic Temple the following Monday morning. Brother Richardson had a third degree confirmed on him at the Ionic Temple when the storm started whipping itself up November 27, 1905. He died a mason of the thirty-second degree, "and his life exemplified the high principles of the Order." He was survived by Dorothy, his wife, and his son, James. He is buried at the Forest Hill Cemetery in Duluth.

Richardson had arrived on the Duluth scene the same year—1898—that Murdoch McLennan began his twenty-six-year stint as captain of Duluth's Life-Saving Service. His crew's inability to save the nine men who perished on the *Mataafa* was always a sore point—even though government investigators vindicated McLennan's actions in their official report. McLennan died at age sixty-eight of kidney and prostate problems, twenty months after Coulby and six months before Richardson. Unlike the weatherman's front-page sendoff, McLennan's passing was condensed to one paragraph on page 5 of the *Duluth News Tribune*. He lies buried in the same Forest Hill cemetery as Richardson.

V

"One after another the famous mines close down as steam shovels bite bottom in the yawning pits."

~ Walter Havighurst, 1966

The first of the steam-powered vessels splashed through the Great Lakes in the 1820s. The Soo Canal opened Lake Superior's big basin to commercial potential in the 1850s. Duluth rose to prominence as one of the world's busiest ports by the early 1900s.

But by the 1960s, the boom was fading. Fast. Although tonnage kept climbing, 1963 found the Lake Carriers' Association reporting the fewest number of steamers on Lake Superior since the century began. U.S. shipyards slipped toward dormant, punched in the gut by Canadian officials' 1961 offer of 40 percent subsidies to ship owners using Canadian-built vessels.

International competition didn't help. By the mid-1960s, American deckhands earned $400 a month, rivaling captains' pay on international ships. One British freighter, flying under a Liberian flag, was paying Chinese sailors fifty cents a day.

The famous Minnesota Iron Range mines of Mesabi and Vermilion became tapped out after a century of what Father Hennepin predicted back in 1679 would be "inconceivable commerce." Taconite pellets would still fuel blast furnaces, but only through a tedious, less-profitable process than the strip-mining and shipping days of yore.

In 1962, the *William Edenborn* was towed to Cleveland and anchored off East 55th Street. Fifty-seven years earlier, the 478-foot steamer had run aground near Gold Rock, losing its barge *Madeira* to the nearby lake bottom. Now it was the *Edenborn*'s turn. Officials sank it and the freighter *James J. Hill*, to serve as breakwaters off Cleveland's east harbor. Together, they formed a thousand-foot wall.

Other ships from the 1905 storm were yanked off the rocks, patched up at hefty prices climbing into the six figures, and floated back into service on the Great Lakes.

Six months after the *Crescent City*'s crewmembers prayed for their souls and crept down a rickety ladder to shore, salvors found a ten-inch gouge just aft of amidships, running down the ship's sides. In the spring of 1906, they pulled the hull free for a $100,000 renovation and a return to the Lakes.

Like many of its old peers, the *Crescent City* was retrofitted from its days as an ore hauler to ferry automobiles across the slate waters of the Inland Seas.

Some things hadn't changed, though. On November 11, 1940, the famous Armistice Day storm found the *Crescent City* fifteen miles northeast of Devil's Island. According to the ship's log book: "The wind flattened out and it stopped raining. After fifteen minutes of calm it started to blow great guns from the north."

The barometer plummeted. The snow fell so thick that the smokestack was impossible to see from the forecastle. Swinging through the arching troughs of Lake Superior, the ship tossed thirty-six cars off the top deck. At 5 a.m. on November 12, 1940, the *Crescent City* sighted Split Rock Lighthouse from its perch 178 feet up on the cliff top. Regaining its bearings, the forty-three-year-old boat limped and crawled its way into Duluth Harbor three hours later. Whether the Split Rock Light and fog signal changed the dynamics of the ship's fate from its shore-crashing thirty-five years earlier, no one knows.

Nine years later, the *Crescent City* was renamed the *Carl W. Meyers*, but its luck didn't change. It collided with a tanker named the *Blue Comet* on December 13, 1950, in Michigan, spilling 84,000 gallons of gas into the Detroit River. In June 1959, some sixty-two years after Augustus Wolvin commissioned its construction at the Chicago

Shipbuilding Company on the city's South Side, the *Crescent City* was towed to Hamilton, Ontario, and torn apart to be sold for scrap steel.

VI

"It looked like it had been worked over with a can opener."

~ Duluth diver George Hovland, 1955

In 1955, a club of young diving enthusiasts zipped themselves into thick wet suits, strapped air tanks on their backs, and jumped into the numbing 45-degree water of Lake Superior north of Two Harbors. They called themselves, fittingly enough, the Frigid Frogs and ranged in age from fourteen to twenty.

They started out a half-mile north of Split Rock Lighthouse, entering the chilly water from a little beach and swimming about one hundred yards north to Gold Rock cliff.

Thousands of divers each year now follow the same route. After a long surface swim, they drop under the surface into icebox conditions nearly devoid of plant life. Picking their way around submerged boulders, they catch a glimpse of a shadowy dark mass. Some divers gulp in a metallic breath of oxygenated air. Others pause, wide-eyed.

Here lurks the bow of the barge *Madeira*, dashed on the rocks in the early morning blizzard of November 28, 1905. The bow points straight up. Its steel shell is torn like a tin can. This is the barge First Mate James Morrow fell from and died. And the one Scandinavian seaman Fred Benson, rope in hand, jumped from before spidering his way up Gold Rock—enduring frozen wave after frozen wave and then dropping the rope down to help save the rest of the crew.

The anchors had been salvaged and put on display at a trading post on Highway 61 and a Great Lakes museum. But in the underwater museum, the holes in the bow are large enough for divers to crawl through, placing the massive shipwreck into human scale. Swimming around the bow, in forty feet of water, divers kick past ladders and hatchways.

The barge's stern, sprawled on its side, sits separated in sixty-five feet of water. A winch wound with steel cable, as large as the divers examining it, lays well-preserved in the chilled water. A similar line connected the powerless barge to its consort, the *William Edenborn*—now the breakwater in Cleveland's harbor. Some say *Edenborn* master A. J. Talbot cut the barge loose to save his ship. Others say the line snapped.

About eight feet down, around the curved rear end of the barge, the large fantail that hung high over the water now hangs over the white, sandy lake bottom. Across a stretch of sand, three sides of

Divers haul up the wheel from the sunken barge *Madeira*, near the spot where Split Rock Lighthouse stands today. *Great Lakes Marine Collection of the Milwaukee Public Library/Wisconsin Marine Historical Society*

the pilot house sit alone in twenty-five feet of water. The waves of November 28, 1905, sheered the pilot house clean off deck, shedding its roof and one side. The corroded compass binnacle sits likes a coffee table in the wreckage of the pilot house.

The middle of the barge is the largest section left, but it doesn't rest between the bow and stern. The stormy collision snapped the ship like a twig and scattered the midsection thirty feet from Gold Rock. From there it plunges one hundred feet deep. Expert divers can enter its hatchway and poke around where its three masts once stood and explore the portholes below.

When it was built in 1901, the *Madeira* ran 436 feet. Divers kicking their flippers along its midsection take an eerily long time to traverse what's left of its once hefty length.

The Frigid Frogs were among the first to dive the *Madeira* wreckage. They had hoped to find treasure but found only a brass porthole wing nut. A week later, in thirty-five feet of water, they came upon the wreckage of the *Lafayette* off Encampment Island some twenty miles to the southwest. Diver Jack Harrom of Duluth plucked an 1860s-style Winchester rifle from the wreck. Amazingly, it still worked. Despite a banged-up barrel, it clicked on its first try and still harbored eleven .44-caliber shells in its magazine and one in its chamber.

An old-timer on the North Shore told the divers it must have belonged to Captain Dell Wright. About the same time the *Edenborn* and its barge, *Madeira*, were striking the rocky shore of Gold Rock, the 454-foot *Lafayette* and its consort barge, *Manila*, were ramming broadside into the cliffs six miles northeast of Two Harbors.

The barge crew climbed trees, and the *Lafayette* engineer grabbed a nut and a rope to rescue all but Patrick Wade, who fell and died during the hand-over-hand climb to shore. Many of the sailors suffered frostbite during the two days it took some local fishermen to get to Two Harbors and convince the tug *Edna G.* to hurry up the North Shore. The *Manila* had been easily refloated. But it took salvors until the next summer to pull up 150 feet of the *Lafayette*'s stern, engine and boilers intact. That was only one-third of the ship, though. Harry Coulby had written it off as a $300,000 loss for U.S. Steel's Pittsburgh Steamship Company.

Captain Wright had left his gun, though, and the old-timers told the Frigid Frogs that sailing crews could be pretty rugged in 1905, and the captain needed some firepower to back up his orders.

In 1960, a guy named Lee Opheim bought the sunken *Madeira* from the Pittsburgh Steamship Company for salvage rights. He sold the anchor to a trading post, and the pilot house wheel now sits on display in a museum in Superior, Wisconsin. In 1992, the *Madeira* landed on the National Register of Historic Places, and nearly one thousand people per year visit its underwater resting place just north of Split Rock Lighthouse.

VII

"Capt. Humble was obliged to leave his boat at Duluth."

~ *Sanilac Jeffersonian*, Sanilac County, Michigan
June 16, 1916

Captain Dick Humble was in the middle of Lake Superior on June 7, 1916, mastering the steamer *Percival Roberts Jr.* It was the fifth boat he'd captained in the eleven years since his *Mataafa* stranded off the Duluth pier.

He was forty-three years old and in horrible pain. His guts were a mess. Shortly after the *Mataafa* disaster, chronic ulcers had started burning holes in his stomach and intestinal lining.

When the *Roberts* whistled into the Duluth harbor, threading between the extended stone piers, Humble was quickly shuttled to St. Luke's Hospital. He died at 9:15 on the night of June 14, 1916.

The coroner who signed his death certificate attributed his passing to a perforation of an ulcer of the duodenum, or the first portion of the small intestine. A ten-year chronic ulcer was listed as a contributory cause of death. His body was then handed over to John Crawford, the Duluth undertaker. Ten-and-a-half years earlier, Crawford had tended to the headless torso that washed up on the Duluth beach when the Thanksgiving storm began to whip the waves into a cauldron.

Arrangements were promptly made to ship Humble's body, one more time, back to Lexington, his hometown on the thumb of Michigan and the shore of Lake Huron. When he was eight years old, an early-morning gale had swept up from the southwest during an arid summer drought and torched the heavily forested region. The 1881 Great Fire burned a million acres in one day, killing 282 people before it burned itself out. To young Richard Humble, this catastrophe must have mirrored the jolt Hurricane Katrina delivered to the children of New Orleans. Old people and children were burned alive. In Delaware Township, where Humble grew up on his father's farm, the Richmond family had jumped in a well and covered it with planks and boards. The next day, neighbors found the burned boards dropped in the well. The top of the father's head was burned off. His wife and five children were dead, twisted around him. A baby, less than a year old, drowned in the two feet of well water. The oldest son, a twelve-year-old, had been at a neighbor's and survived.

When it came to nightmares, one wonders whether Humble tossed and turned more from the flashbacks of fire or the icy cold of November 28, 1905. Whether his ulcers were fueled by his memories or the drink that soothed them is anyone's guess.

When his casket arrived in Lexington, his wife, Jessie, was waiting with the three children, all under ten years old. Jessie Hunt, too, had grown up in Lexington. She was the daughter of a wagon maker. She had lived through the fires and must have instructed Crawford to send his body home, even though they now lived on the shores of Lake Erie in Conneaut, Ohio.

They'd married in 1902 at Jessie's mother's home in Lexington and settled across the Lakes in Conneaut, Ohio. Jessie worked as an artist there, decorating china. Her graceful touch, for years, led her to hand-letter the Conneaut school diplomas until the process became mechanized.

The three children promptly appeared following the Humbles' move to Ohio. Bernice was born in the months before the *Mataafa* tragedy in 1905. Blanche arrived in 1907, and Richard was born in 1910—at least the third male Humble with that name. Bernice and Blanche never married and lived together on the upscale Overlook Road in one of Cleveland's nicer areas. Although their father died when they were girls, he apparently left them on solid financial footing. Blanche taught school in Cleveland Heights, and Bernice was a sales clerk at a Cleveland department store. When their mother died in 1928, little Richie was eighteen. Although his memories of his father were dim—he was six when his dad died—he followed in Dick Humble's footsteps and went to sea at an early age.

The young Richard Humble's name starts showing up on ship manifests when he was eighteen. He was living on South Street in New York City in July 1942, sailing with the Merchant Marines on the U.S.

freighter *Tachira* in the Caribbean Sea. A torpedo sank the ship and killed Captain Humble's only son at age thirty-two. That's the same age of Captain Humble when he mastered the *Mataafa* in the 1905 storm.

The *Mataafa* would outlast both Humbles. It had taken more than six months before salvors refloated the boat off the Duluth rocks in 1906. After costly repairs, the ship that Gus Wolvin had originally commissioned in 1898 went on sailing for six decades.

The *Mataafa* had a 1908 collision with the *Sacramento* and at least one fire and another boat-to-boat crash. In the spring of 1960, the *Mataafa* was refitted for automobile transportation, providing car ferry service for five hundred vehicles daily between Detroit and Buffalo. In 1965, the *Mataafa* rode under its own power for the last time before being towed to Hamburg, Germany, where it was scrapped.

In the Marine News column of the *Duluth News Tribune* on June 15, 1916, a single paragraph shared the news of Captain Humble's death the day before. To the end, his fate was tied to that of the *Mataafa*:

"Captain Humble was well known to all the marine men on the lakes, and will be remembered as the commander of the ill-fated *Mataafa*, which was wrecked off this port in the winter of 1905."

In the next paragraph, which detailed the arrivals and departures of the Lake Superior fleet, it was reported that the *Mataafa* had sailed between the outstretched piers and into Duluth harbor at 10:35 the morning after Humble's death.

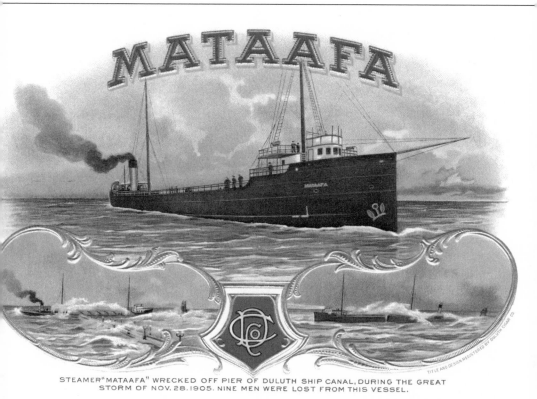

STEAMER "MATAAFA" WRECKED OFF PIER OF DULUTH SHIP CANAL, DURING THE GREAT
STORM OF NOV. 28. 1905. NINE MEN WERE LOST FROM THIS VESSEL.

The Duluth Cigar Company came out with a commemorative *Mataafa* cigar
box after the tragic storm. *Great Lakes Marine Collection of the Milwaukee
Public Library/Wisconsin Marine Historical Society*

Acknowledgments

My cell phone shook one day on the sidelines of my son's soccer game. It was Maryjane Honner, calling from Sterling, Michigan, on the bay in Lake Huron. I was talking to the great-great-niece of Captain Thomas Honner, thanks to an amazing website with a self-deprecating address: www.boatnerd.com. Honner, the classy veteran master, had agreed to haul a run of barley on the *Ira H. Owen* because Captain Joseph Hulligan had taken ill. Maryjane's tireless research and expertise added depth to this project.

Maryjane led her long-lost uncle, Tom Honore, my way. His family changed the spelling of its name back to the French "Honore" after Tom's grandfather went down at the helm of the *Owen*. Born along Lake Michigan in Kenosha, Wisconsin, Tom Honore was a long-time architect in California and Arizona and now lives in the Blue Ridge Mountains of Virginia. He sent along Captain Thomas Honner's memorial service program and the letter from Captain Gale.

John Belliveau, another voice from boatnerd.com, was kind enough to visit the Detroit office of the J. W. Westcott Company. The firm provided mail in a pail, originally using rowboats to deliver mail to the big freighters. Crewmembers would lower pails on ropes from the deck and pull back the mail of the day. John Belliveau and John Ward Westcott II scoured the company archives and found a photo album filled with images from the *Mataafa* in 1904—the year before its fateful night in Duluth.

Others of immeasurable help include:

Laura Jacobs at the University of Wisconsin–Superior, who sent an inches-thick stack of crisply copied old storm clippings from the Duluth newspapers. Said one of her e-mails: "Boy, is it easy to get sucked into THIS project!"

Tracey Baker and the rest of the crew at the Minnesota Historical Society.

Al Miller, whose e-mails and book, *Tin Stackers: The History of the Pittsburgh Steamship Company*, enriched my understanding.

Robert W. Graham, archivist of the Historical Collection of the Great Lakes at Bowling Green University.

Sean Ley, Thomas L. Farnquist, and Steve Daniel of the Great Lakes Shipwreck Historical Society.

Ken Merryman of the Great Lakes Shipwreck Preservation Society.

Jennifer MacLeod of the Marsh Collection Society in Amherstburg, Ontario, where the *Mataafa*'s two black storm victims lived.

St. Paul historian Jim Sazevich.

Mary McFadden's niece Patricia Partridge.

Patricia Maus at the Northeast Minnesota Historical Society at the University of Minnesota–Duluth.

College of St. Catherine librarian Kathi Rickert.

Encouraging editor Danielle Ibister.

And friend and publisher Michael Dregni, who wanted to hear the story and made this telling possible.

Appendix

Alphabetical roster of the boats on Lake Superior during the *Mataafa* storm of November 27 through 29, 1905:

1.   AMBOY: Three-masted schooner-barge that ran aground on the beach three miles northeast of the Manitou River, along with the steamer towing it, the *George Spencer*. The thirty-one-year-old boat, built in 1874, was bound for Duluth with a load of coal. Lines were tossed and retrieved by fishermen. Watchman James Gibson swung hand-over-hand for 150 feet and helped fishermen and lumberjacks set up the chair buoy. All survived, led to shore by the trip's substitute steward, Mrs. Harry Lawe, the mate's wife. Settlers in Thomasville took them in. A total loss, estimated at $10,000, after the boat was left to break into pieces.

2. ANGELINE: Caught in mid-Superior, with waves higher than its smokestack, the 414-foot steamer made it to the Soo Canal with minor topside damage.

3. ARIZONA: One of the oldest, smallest, and luckiest boats caught in the storm, the 189-foot wooden hooker spun wildly in stiff winds a quarter-mile out of the Duluth Ship Canal. Wound up bow first and in safe harbor November 28. One of the few times fate smiled on it. The *Arizona* sank in an 1873 collision in twenty-four feet of water. Raised and repaired only to catch fire in Marquette, Michigan, in 1887. In 1922, the *Arizona* caught fire and burned to a total loss at age fifty-four.

4. BRANSFORD: Scraped a reef southwest of Isle Royale's Menagerie Island. Some fancy maneuvering from Captain C. C. Balfour, who backed the 414-foot steel steamer off the reef until a giant wave released it for a long limp to Duluth. It arrived with seventy-seven cracks and punctures, costing Hawgood Shipping $15,000. Said Balfour: "I'm willing to go on record saying that in my experience all gales that I've witnessed were Fourth of July zephyrs compared with that blow on Lake Superior."

5. CONSTITUTION: The runaway 452-foot steel barge broke loose from its consort, *Victory*, off Copper Harbor, careening with faulty steering some 120 miles to the Porcupine

Mountains shoreline. A fishing company's 124-foot wooden packet steamer *C. W. Moore* grabbed control of the barge, later submitting a $10,000 bill for the rescue.

6. CORALIA: Another in the string of Pittsburgh Steamships out on Lake Superior, the 413-foot steel steamer struck hard on the eastern edge of Keweenaw Point but was easily refloated.

7. WILLIAM E. COREY: The largest and youngest member of the Pittsburgh Steamship armada, the 558-foot, 6,363-ton monster named after U.S. Steel's new boss snared itself on the rocks of Gull Island Reef in the Apostle Islands. With Pittsburgh Steamship President Harry Coulby onsite to supervise, several large ships took a dozen days to yank it loose for a $100,000 repair.

8. CRESCENT CITY: Built in 1897, the 406-foot member of the Pittsburgh Steamship fleet slipped between jutting rocks one mile east of the Duluth pumping station near Lakewood. The entire crew climbed down a rickety ladder to a low cliff. Hauled off the shore in 1906, overhauled for $100,000, and eventually retrofitted into a car ferry.

9. WILLIAM EDENBORN: Third assistant engineer James Johnson died when he was knocked off his feet into a hatch wrenched open as the ship began to crack. The five-year-old Pittsburgh

Steamship's 478-footer lost its tether with its barge, *Madeira*, which broke up and sank at Gold Rock cliff nearby. Months later, salvors pulled it free from the mouth of the Split Rock River for a $100,000 overhaul.

10. ISAAC L. ELLWOOD: Careened off the north and south piers of the Duluth Ship Canal before settling in twenty feet of water near the Duluth Boat Club. The 478-foot Pittsburgh Steamship drew hearty applause from onlookers just before the *Mataafa* failed to run the same gauntlet. Renovated for $50,000.

11. R. W. ENGLAND: Only a year old, the 363-foot steel steamer missed the Duluth Ship Canal and was blown stern-first on the Park Point beach some two miles south of Duluth. The lifesaving crew scrambled to the scene, saving the crew from little risk and causing the lifesavers to be out of position when the *Mataafa* crashed into the pier soon after. The repair bill on the $230,000 boat ran over $70,000.

12. GEORGE HERBERT: Three Duluth sailors—Ole Miller, George Olson, and Ole Nelson—refused to jump when their flat-bottom wooden scow, towed by the tugboat *F. W. Gillett*, splintered on the rocks near Two Islands, some eighty miles up the North Shore from Duluth. They were bringing supplies to a lumber camp. All three men died.

13. **LAFAYETTE:** Fireman Patrick Wade died when he slipped from the line down which the others swung hand-over-hand to safety six miles northeast of Two Harbors near Encampment Island. The 454-foot steamer rammed a bluff and its barge, *Manila*, piled into its stern, allowing four crewmembers a way off the *Lafayette*. Only 150 feet of its stern was salvaged after the boat split in two. The quadruple-expansion engine was intact and placed in another ship in 1909.

14. **MADEIRA:** Three-masted, steel schooner-barge that crashed northeast of Split Rock. The 436-footer lost its connection with consort *Edenborn* and broke up at the base of Gold Rock cliff. Seaman Fred Benson jumped to the cliff, scrambled up, and tossed a rope down to save all but mate James Morrow. Morrow tried climbing a mast to jump, changed his mind, and was washed away when the barge split in two. The wrecked ship remains a popular diving spot.

15. **MAIA:** Consort barge with the *Coralia*, the 387-foot steel vessel ran ashore near Point Abbaye on the eastern shore of the Keweenaw Peninsula. Easily returned to service for the Pittsburgh Steamship fleet.

16. **MANILA:** The 436-foot barge crashed ashore with consort steamer *Lafayette* six miles northeast of Two Harbors. The

Manila wound up along the *Lafayette*'s stern underneath overhanging trees and a low-lying cliff. Crewmembers climbed the trees to scramble to safety and help rescue all but one of the *Lafayette*'s crew. The shipwrecked sailors were able to return to the *Manila* when the storm eased, finding heat and food until help arrived from Two Harbors. Crewmembers suffered frostbite, but the barge was easily returned to service for $10,000.

17. **MARIPOSA:** The deck damage suffered on the open Lake Superior during the storm wasn't the first trouble in 1905 for the Pittsburgh Steamship's 330-footer. Back in May, it got caught in the ice and was rammed by the steamer *Admiral*.

18. **MATAAFA:** Six members of the crew—fireman Thomas Woodgate, deckhand Thomas McCloud, engineer William Most, steward Henry Wright, oiler Carl Carlson, and cook Walter Bush—died from exposure to cold and waves when the 429-foot steamer was stranded off the Duluth piers. Three others—oiler William Gilchrist and assistant engineers C. A. Farenger and James Early—were washed away and drowned. Captain Richard Humble and fourteen others up front survived, some thanks to daring dashes up the deck between waves while thousands of Duluthians watched on from burning bonfires only a few hundred yards away. After a

The *Mataafa* gets towed under the new aerial bridge in Duluth. *Milwaukee Public Library*

$100,000 salvage in 1906, the *Mataafa* was back on the Lakes until 1964, finishing its life as an auto ferry.

19. MONKSHAVEN: After twenty-two years as an ocean vessel, the British-built 249-foot steel turret steamer was the storm's first victim up on the Canadian North Shore about a dozen miles from Thunder Bay. The crew climbed off the bow to a nearby island.

20. HAROLD B. NYE: Mate William Sturtevant was washed overboard near Outer Island as the 380-footer suffered extensive damage near the Apostle Islands. When it eventually limped into

Two Harbors, crewmembers reported seeing a boat matching the description of the *Ira H. Owen* before it foundered.

21. IRA H. OWEN: All nineteen aboard died when the 262-foot twin-stacker foundered with a light load of barley heading from Duluth to Buffalo. Captain Joseph Hulligan had taken ill, so another Great Lakes veteran, Thomas Honner, was at the helm when it was lost off Outer Island in the Apostles. It was last seen blowing its distress whistle, and wreckage was found near Michigan Island, including life rings printed with the boat's name.

22. E. C. POPE: The 323-footer drew applause from the Duluth crowds when it sailed through the piers with sections of its fore cabin carried away, a hole in its bow, and the steering damaged. "She dodged like a frightened animal when she went into the waters at the mouth of the canal," the *Duluth News Tribune* reported November 29, 1905.

23. S. C. REYNOLDS: The 255-footer was safely tied to the Duluth dock but caused $500 damage and became a fixture in law books after a famous case about property liability for harm caused by necessity. It was eventually sunk by a German torpedo in World War I.

24. ROSEMOUNT: The 244-foot Canadian package freighter was marooned off Thunder Bay but later salvaged.

25. GEORGE SPENCER: A 231-foot wooden bulk freighter built in 1884, it was among the first ore ships sailing from Two Harbors. Grounded three miles northeast of the Manitou River near Thomasville some seventy miles up the North Shore from Duluth. Its coal was retrieved and the boat sailed again, unlike its barge, *Amboy*, which broke up and whose wreckage was placed on the National Register of Historical Places in 1994 after divers photographed its remains.

26. UMBRIA: The new 420-footer arrived in Duluth stripped of its pilot house with its steering barely working. Said Second Mate Andrew Cornaliusan: "A hundred times while we struggled with the gearing, the hopelessness of the effort chilled my heart."

27. PERRY G. WALKER: An ore-ladened 416-footer that saw its "cabin get turned into matchwood" on the open lake, according to a crewmember. It came to port with a tarp covering its pilot house and all of its furniture gone.

28. WESTERN STAR: Blown 125 miles off course, the 416-foot steel steamer beached on shore at Fourteen Mile Point near

Ontonagon, Michigan, west of Keweenaw Point. The little steamer *Viking* pulled it free, not counting the $20,000 repair tab.

29. YOSEMITE: The 356-foot new steel steamer suffered damage on the open lake but made it to Duluth "with its bridge hanging like the wing of a wounded duck," according to newspaper accounts.

In Memoriam

Here is a partial, alphabetical list of those who died in the 1905 storm on Lake Superior. The names of eight crewmembers of the *Ira H. Owen* were never reported.

1. J. P. Alger, second engineer, *Ira H. Owen.*
2. H. Buchanan, engineer, *Ira H. Owen.*
3. Walter Bush, *Mataafa* cook, Amherstburg, Ontario.
4. Oliver Campbell, deckhand, *Ira H. Owen.*
5. Carl Carlson, *Mataafa* oiler, Chicago.
6. James Early, *Mataafa* third engineer, Buffalo.
7. C. A. Farenger, *Mataafa* second engineer, Cleveland.
8. William Gilchrist, *Mataafa* oiler, Wiarton, Ontario.
9. M. Haggerty, second mate on the *Ira H. Owen.*
10. Thomas Honner, first mate and fill-in captain on the *Ira H. Owen.*
11. N. Hook, oiler, *Ira H. Owen.*
12. Joseph Hulligan, *Ira H. Owen* captain who'd taken ill.
13. J. Jacobson, wheelman, *Ira H. Owen.*
14. James Johnson, third engineer on *William Edenborn*, fell into an open hatch.

15.   J. Knudson, lookout, *Ira H. Owen.*

16.   Thomas McCloud, *Mataafa* deckhand,
Brandenburg, Kentucky.

17.   C. McKay, lookout, *Ira H. Owen.*

18.   Ole Miller, sailor on the scow *George Herbert.*

19.   L. Montray, wheelman, *Ira H. Owen.*

20.   James Morrow, mate on the *Madeira*, went overboard.

21.   William Most, *Mataafa* engineer Cleveland.

22.   Ole Nelson, sailor on the scow *George Herbert.*

23.   George Olson, sailor on the scow *George Herbert.*

24.   William Sturtevant, a mate on the *Harold B. Nye*, was
washed off the deck.

25.   Patrick Wade, *Lafayette* fireman slipped from the line
as others swung hand-over-hand to safety.

26.   Thomas Woodgate, *Mataafa* fireman, Toronto.

27.   Henry Wright, *Mataafa* steward, Amherstburg, Ontario.

References

Books

Barry, James P. *Ships of the Great Lakes: 300 Years of Navigation.* Lansing, Michigan: Thunder Bay Press, 1973.

Barry, James P. *Wrecks and Rescues of the Great Lakes.* Lansing, Michigan: Thunder Bay Press, 1994.

Berger, Todd R. *Lighthouses of the Great Lakes.* Stillwater, Minnesota: Voyageur Press, 2002.

Bowen, Dana Thomas. *Memories of the Lakes.* Cleveland, Ohio: Freshwater Press, 1969.

Brown, David G. *White Hurricane, A Great Lakes November Gale and America's Deadliest Maritime Disaster.* United States: McGraw-Hill Companies, 2002.

Curwood, Oliver James. *The Great Lakes, The Vessels That Plough Them: Their Owners, Their Sailors, and Their Cargoes.* New York and London: The Knickerbocker Press, 1909.

Feltner, Charles E. and Jeri Baron Felton. *Great Lakes Maritime History: Bibliography and Sources of Information.* Dearborn, Michigan: Seajay Publications, 1982.

Havighurst, Walter, ed. *The Great Lakes Reader*. New York: MacMillan, 1966.

Havighurst, Walter. *Vein of Iron, The Pickands Mather Story*. Cleveland: World Publishing Company, 1958.

Knott, Leanne Denise. *The Keeper's Daughter*. Lincoln, Nebraska: iUniverse, 2006.

LesStrang, Jacques. *Lake Carriers: The Saga of the Great Lakes Fleet*. Seattle: Salisbury Press, 1977.

Miller, Al. *Tin Stackers: The History of the Pittsburgh Steamship Company*. Detroit: Wayne State University Press, 1999.

Mills, James. *Our Inland Seas*, Cambridge: A.C. McClurg, 1910.

Quick, Herbert. *American Inland Waterways*. New York: The Knickerbocker Press, 1909.

Ratigan, William. *Great Lakes Shipwrecks and Survivals*. New York: Galahad Books, 1960.

Richardson, H. W. *The Climate of Duluth, Minnesota*. Duluth: Commercial Club, 1914.

Thompson, Mark L. *Graveyards of the Lakes*. Detroit: Wayne State University Press, 2006.

Wolff, Julius F., Jr. *Lake Superior Shipwrecks*. Duluth: Lake Superior Port Cities, 1990.

Periodicals, Pamphlets, Government Documents

Captain Humble's notarized 1905 statement. Lake Superior Marine Museum Association Collection, University of Wisconsin–Superior.

Coleman, Herbert J. "Divers Find Superior's Floor is Underwater Scrap Yard." *Lake Carriers' Association Bulletin*. September 1955.

Onlookers stand watch for loved ones at the Duluth pier. *J. W. Westcott Co. Archives*

Gebhart, Richard. "The Three Hardest Voyages in the 62 Years of the *Crescent City.*" *Inland Seas.* Spring 1991: 26–32.

History of St. Louis County, 1910.

Holden, Thom. "Wicked November Storms." *Lake Superior Magazine.* October–November 1990: 35–41.

Keller, James. "The Madeira." *Inland Seas.* Summer 1983.

Lake Carriers' Association. *Annual Report.* 1905.

Lake Carriers' Association. "History of the Iron Ore Trade." *Annual Report.* 1910.

Lapinski, Patrick. "Chasing Underwater Shadows." *Lake Superior Magazine.* October–November 2007: 23–31.

LeMay, Konnie. "For Those in Peril on the Sea: A Century after a Storm of the Century." *Lake Superior Magazine.* October–November 2005: 16–23.

Mack, Stanley L. *History of the Ionic Lodge No. 186*. Duluth,
     April 1931.

Miller, Al. "Teeming with Enterprise: Augustus B. Wolvin's Life on
     the Great Lakes." *Inland Seas*. Spring 2002: 7–27.

Minnesota Department of Transportation. *Great Lakes
     Transportation*. St. Paul, 1989.

Minnesota Federation of Architects and Engineers. *Herbert
     Richardson Biography*. May 1931.

Minnesota Historical Society. *Split Rock Lighthouse*. Minnesota
     Historic Sites Series.

Minnesota Historical Society. *Split Rock: Epoch of a Lighthouse*.

Sugarman, Stephen D. *Vincent v. Lake Erie Transportation: Liability
     for Harm Caused by Necessity*.

United States Life-Saving Service. *Annual Report, Fiscal Year Ended
     June 30*. Washington: Government Printing Office, 1906.

"Weather Service to the Northland." National Weather Service, Duluth.

Newspapers

The author relied heavily on the *Duluth News Tribune* and the
Duluth Evening Herald in the weeks surrounding November 27,
1905. Here are some other newspaper credits:

Boxmeyer, Don. "Tracing a Superior Mystery: The Final Hours of the
     Fitz." *St. Paul Pioneer Press*. November 10, 2006.

Brown, Curt. "An Irish lass with sass: Mary McFadden." *Minneapolis
     Star Tribune*. March 17, 2004.

"Georgian Triangle: Shipwrecks of the Great Lakes." *Enterprise
     Bulletin*. September 23, 2003.

Humble Wedding and Death Information. *Sanilac (Mich.) Jeffersonian*. December 26, 1902, and June 16, 1916.

"Many Union Sailors Are Lost in the Storm." *The (Duluth) Labor World*. December 2, 1905.

Marine Review. December 7, 1905.

Marquette (Mich.) Daily Mining Journal. November 28, 1905.

"Mary McFadden, News Veteran Dies." *Minneapolis Daily Times*. May 30, 1944. p. 9.

Oakes, Larry. "The Mystery of the *Edmund Fitzgerald*." *Star Tribune*. November 10, 1997.

Spokesman Review. Spokane, Washington.

"Went Down With His Ship." *Grand Haven (Michigan) Daily Tribune*. December 2, 1905.

Other Library and Web-based Resources

Great Lakes Vessels Index, Historical Collections of the Great Lakes. Bowling Green State University.

Milwaukee Public Library Ship Information and Data Record

Minnesota Historical Society, Minnesota's Lake Superior Shipwrecks, History of Minnesota's Lake Superior, www.mnhs.org.

William H. Aitkin Memorial Library, Sanliac County, Michigan

www.boatnerd.com

www.cityofwickliffe.com

www.lakefury.com

www.rootsweb.com

Index

Index

About the Author

Author Curt Brown is a staff writer with the *Minneapolis Star Tribune*. A general assignment reporter, Brown has worked at the paper for twenty years. A history buff with a B.A. in American history, he's been researching the 1905 Thanksgiving storm on Lake Superior for five years. Brown lives in St. Paul, Minnesota, with his wife, Adele. They have three children.

Photograph © Kyndell Harkness

ONTARIO

Thunder Bay ● ⊠ Rosemount

⊠ Monkshaven

Isle Royal

⊠ Bransford

Grand Marais ●

MINNESOTA

LAKE

⊠ Amboy
⊠ George Spencer
Split Rock ■ ⊠ George Herbert
⊠ Madeira
William Edenborn

⊠ Harold B. Nye

⊠ Ira H. Owen

Two Harbors ● ⊠ Manila
⊠ Lafayette

William E.
Corey ⊠

Western
Star
⊠

Duluth ●
⊠ Crescent City

APOSTLE ISLANDS

Superior ●

Bayfield ●

● Ontonagon

Mataafa
R.W. England
Isaac L. Ellwood
Arizona
S.C. Reynolds

Ashland ●

PORCUPINE MTS.

UNITED

WISCONSIN